365 Days of Walking the Red Road

The Native American Path to
Leading a Spiritual Life Every Day

Terri Jean

D0504063

Adams Media

New York   London   Toronto   Sydney   New Delhi

This book is dedicated to my mother
for teaching me how to write, and to my
great-grandmother, Whitlatch, for all of
her inspiration and encouragement.

Adams Media
An Imprint of Simon & Schuster, Inc.
100 Technology Center Drive
Stoughton, MA 02072

Copyright © 2003 by Terri Jean.

For information about special discounts for bulk purchases,
please contact Simon & Schuster Special Sales at 1-866-506-1949
or business@simonandschuster.com.

The Simon & Schuster Speakers Bureau can bring authors to your live
event. For more information or to book an event contact the Simon &
Schuster Speakers Bureau at 1-866-248-3049 or visit our website at
www.simonspeakers.com.

Interior photographs courtesy of © Corel, © 1999 PhotoDisc, Inc., and
© 1998 Digital Stock Corp.

Manufactured in Canada

24 25 26 MAR 31 30 29

Library of Congress Cataloging-in-Publication Data has been applied for.

ISBN 978-1-58062-849-5

Acknowledgments

I would like to acknowledge the effort, energy, and education of the many people who believed in my work, my writing, and my convictions. To those family, friends, and mentors who supported me unconditionally, I appreciate your kindness, patience, and time. And to those who unselfishly chose to educate me on their Native history, issues, culture, and experiences, thank you. Without you, this book would not be possible.

Introduction

O' Great Spirit help me always to speak the truth quietly, to listen with an open mind when others speak, and to remember the peace that may be found in silence.

—CHEROKEE PRAYER

When one is walking the Red Road, one is living as instructed by the Creator. The person who walks the Red Road lives a life of truth and charity—values handed down generation to generation. Though the road is littered with obstacles, all can be overcome once internal balance is achieved and the soul is true to itself and to others.

This book is full of such values, and the inspirational speakers span hundreds of years of Native American history. Their philosophies are rich and full of feeling, articulating myriad emotions and cultural instruction. Each quote is a lesson; each speaker is a teacher. The 365 lessons ring with the same wisdom and strength now as they did the day they were spoken.

THE NORTHERN JOURNEY OF WINTER

White covers much of the earth during winter's harsh, cold months, representing the nourishing blanket that secures all of nature while it lies sleeping. Winter also represents elders and their final walks along the Red Road. Our grandparents are wise and the winter is silent. Therefore, the time of the North is a special time for storytelling. In olden times, children and adults would gather around a fire and hear the storyteller narrate legends and myths of their people. Storytellers orally teach the traditions of their people and keep alive the history of their tribe. The Chippewa call North "Waboose," which is depicted as a strong, powerful buffalo withstanding the effects of winter.

Direction: North
Season: Winter
Color: White

From the beginning there were drums,
beating out world rhythm—the
booming, never-failing tide on the
beach; the four seasons, gliding
smoothly, one from the other; when
the birds come, when they go, the bear
hibernating for his winter sleep.
Unfathomable the way, yet all in per-
fect time. Watch the heartbeat in your
wrist—a precise pulsing beat of life's
Drum—with loss of timing you are ill.

—JIMALEE BURTON (HO-CHEE-NEE),
CHEROKEE, 1974

JANUARY

Red Road Ethic 1
Honor the Great Spirit

Every element of creation expresses the Creator. Within each mountain, each stone, and each heart lies the Great Spirit. All are of the Creator, and each particle of the universe is equally deserving of respect and admiration. When looking upon a sunset, the trees, or even your worst enemy, you are looking at the Creator. Know this and give praise and prayer.

A wee child toddling in a wonder world, I prefer to their dogma my excursions into the natural gardens where the voice of the Great Spirit is heard in the twittering of birds, the rippling of mighty waters, and the sweet breathing of flowers. If this is Paganism, then at present, at least, I am a Pagan.

—ZITKALA-SA (GERTRUDE SIMMONS BONNIN OR RED BIRD), SIOUX AUTHOR AND ACTIVIST, 1876–1938

January 1

What is life? It is the flash of a firefly in the night. It is the breath of a buffalo in the wintertime. It is the little shadow which runs across the grass and loses itself in the sunset.

—CROWFOOT,
BLACKFOOT WARRIOR AND ORATOR,
1826–1890

On This Date in Native American History

January 1, 1802: Peter Jones, Mississauga (Ojibway), was born. He later became a Mississauga chief and Methodist missionary, traveling throughout Canada and the United States preaching the gospel and addressing Native issues.

January 2

*I love a people who have always made
me welcome to the best they had . . .
who are honest without laws, who have
no jails and no poor-houses . . . who
never take the name of God in vain . . .
who worship God without a Bible, and
I believe God loves them also . . . who
are free from religious animosities . . .
who have never raised a hand against
me, or stolen my property, where there
is no law to punish either . . . who never
fought a battle with white men except
on their own ground . . . and Oh, how
I love a people who don't live for the love
of money!*

—GEORGE CATLIN
AN AMERICAN NON-NATIVE ARTIST
OF THE 1830S, SPEAKING ABOUT THE
NATIVE PEOPLE HE HAD ENCOUNTERED

January 3

We never did the white man any harm;
we don't intend to . . . we are willing to
be friends with the white man . . .

—HOTOAKHIHOOIS (TALL BULL),
TO GENERAL WINFIELD SCOTT HANCOCK,
MARCH 1867

Did You Know?

The term "crossing over" is common among Native people today to refer to those who died or who are dying.

January 4

Kindness is to use one's will to guard one's speech and conduct so as not to injure anyone.

—ORAL TRADITIONAL
TEACHING OF THE OMAHA

On This Date in
Native American History

January 4, 1975: The Indian Self-Determination and Education Assistance Act was passed by Congress to encourage the development of tribal educational services.

January 5

The earth has received the
embrace of the sun and we
shall see the results of that love.

—HUNKESNI (SITTING BULL),
HUNKPAPA SIOUX, 1831-1890

A Native to Know

Handsome Lake, half brother of Corn-planter, was a spiritual prophet who stressed the importance of traditional religious ceremonies and preached a message that would later be known as the "Code of Handsome Lake." His spiritual messages were heard by many Iroquois people, who traveled for miles to hear him speak. Even after his death in 1815, his teachings continue through his followers and are now known as the Longhouse Religion.

January 6

Often in the stillness of the night when all nature seems asleep about me there comes a gentle rapping at the door of my heart. I open it and a voice inquires, "Pokagon, what of your people? What will their future be?" My answer is: "Mortal man has not the power to draw aside the veil of unborn time to tell the future of his race. That gift belongs of the Divine alone. But it is given to him to closely judge the future by the present, and the past."

—SIMON POKAGON,
POTAWATOMI, 1830–1899

January 7

Everything on the earth has a purpose, every disease an herb to cure it, and every person a mission. This is the Indian theory of existence.

—Mourning Dove
(Christine Quintasket), Salish,
1888–1936

Did You Know?

"Alaska" is a Native word that means "the great country."

January 8

It is well to be good to women in the strength of our manhood because we must sit under their hands at both ends of our lives.

—HE DOG,
OGLALA SIOUX

Did You Know?

Beloved Woman is an important community figure among the Cherokee people. The wise woman bestowed this role acts as a one-woman legal counsel and judicial authority over all members of her tribe. Her word is law and all people must abide.

January 9

*Civilization has been thrust
upon me . . . and it has not
added one whit to my love for
truth, honesty, and generosity.*

—LUTHER STANDING BEAR,
OGLALA SIOUX, 1868–1937

On This Date in
Native American History

January 9, 1789: Treaty of Fort
Harmar was signed.

January 10

The Great Spirit is in all things, he is in the air we breathe. The Great Spirit is our Father, but the Earth is our Mother. She nourishes us, that which we put into the ground she returns to us . . .

—BEDAGI (BIG THUNDER),
WABANAKÍ ALGONQUIN, 1900s

Did You Know?

The Talking Feather is a communication device used by various tribes to ensure a person's right to speak without interruption from others. The leader of the meeting would first hold the Talking Feather, and then pass it around the room or give it to those who requested a turn. The feather typically held a special meaning to that particular tribe, and it would be decorated with distinctive colors and symbols. In other tribal communities, a Talking Stick would be used in the same manner.

January 11

*I have already agreed to be there
and that is the same as if I gave you
my head and my heart . . . I won't
try to take back what I have said.
I will do as I told you I would.*

—WESTERN APACHE TRIBAL MEMBER

On This Date in
Native American History

January 11, 1972: The Reverend Harold
Jones, a South Dakota Sioux, was made
a bishop in the Episcopal Church. He
was the first Native American Indian to
hold this position.

January 12

*Honor the sacred. Honor the Earth—
our Mother. Honor the Elders. Honor
all with whom we share the Earth:
Four-legged, two-legged, winged ones,
swimmers, crawlers, plant and rock
people. Walk in balance and beauty.*

—ANONYMOUS NATIVE AMERICAN ELDER

Did You Know?

For many Native American tribes, certain
colors hold specific and sacred meanings. For example, to the Cherokee, red
and black are two Cardinal Colors worn
at many ceremonies and dances. Red
represents the east, and black the west.
White is for south, while blue symbol-
izes north.

January 13

Among the Indians there have been no written laws. Customs handed down from generation to generation have been the only laws to guide them. Every one might act different from what was considered right, did he choose to do so, but such acts would bring upon him the censure of the Nation . . . This fear of the Nation's censure acted as a mighty band, binding all in one social, honorable compact.

—GEORGE COPWAY,
OJIBWAY CHIEF, 1818–1863

January 14

Why do you take by force what you could obtain by love?

—WAHUNSONACOCK (POWHATAN),
POWHATAN, 1547–1622

On This Date in
Native American History

January 14, 1833: Reverend Samuel Worcester was released from a Georgia prison, after serving four years of hard labor for speaking out against the mistreatment of Cherokee Indians.

Red Road Lesson 1
The Good Red Road

Originally, the term "The Red Road" or "The Good Red Road" was used by the Plains people to signify one's righteous relationship with their divinity.

When one walks the Red Road, one is living within the rules of the Creator, living a life of truth, friendship, respect, spirituality, and humanitarianism. Today, the phrase is shared by numerous people all over the world.

Creator of the world, Maker of all men;
Lord of lords, my eyes fail me . . . for
the sole desire [is] to know thee.

—INCA HYMN

January 15

Let us put our minds together and see what life will make for our children.

—Hunkesni (Sitting Bull),
Hunkpapa Sioux, 1831–1890

A Native to Know

Sitting Bull, known as Tantanka-Iyotanka by his people, was a Hunkpapa Sioux holy man and follower of the Ghost Dance Religion who united his people and fought for survival on the northern plains. His courage was legendary and his tribal convictions made him a beloved and well-respected Native leader.

January 16

I hope the Great Heavenly Father, who will look down upon us, will give all the tribes His blessing, that we may go forth in peace and live in peace all our days, and that he will look down upon our children and finally lift us far above this earth; and that our Heavenly Father will look upon our children as His children, that all the tribes may be His children. And as we shake hands to-day upon this broad plain, we may forever live in peace.

—RED CLOUD (MAKHPIYA-LUTA),
OGLALA SIOUX CHIEF, LATE 19TH CENTURY

January 17

*I cannot think that we are useless
or God would not have created us.*

—GOYATHLAY (GERONIMO),
APACHE MEDICINE MAN AND WAR CHIEF,
1829–1909

In Remembrance

Of Mangas Coloradas, Apache chief,
who died on this date 1863.

January 18

We will bury the tomahawk in the earth.

—SAUK ADAGE MEANT
AS A PLEDGE OF PEACE

On This Date in
Native American History

January 18, 1800: The Peace Preservation Act was passed.

January 19

We preferred hunting to a life of idle-ness on our reservation. At times we did not get enough to eat and we were not allowed to hunt. All we wanted was peace and to be let alone . . . I was not allowed to remain quiet. I was tired of fighting . . . I have spoken.

—CRAZY HORSE,
OGLALA SIOUX, ON HIS DEATHBED, 1877

January 20

I will follow the white man's trail.
I will take him as my friend, but I
will not bend my back to his burdens.
I will be cunning as a coyote. I will
ask him to understand his ways, then
I will prepare the way for my children,
and their children. The Great Spirit
has shown me—a day will come when
they will outrun the white man in his
own shoes.

—MANY HORSES

Did You Know?

That Appaloosa horses, though named by Canadian-French explorers, were developed by the Nez Perce Indians.

January 21

O Great Spirit whose voice I hear in the winds, I come to you as one of your many children. I need your strength and your wisdom. Make me strong not to be superior to my brother, but to be able to fight my greatest enemy: Myself.

—Chief Dan George,
Coast Salish, 1899–1981

On This Date in
Native American History

January 21, 1969: Navajo Community College (now called Diné College), the first all-Indian-operated community college, opened.

January 22

The idea of full dress in preparation for a battle comes not from a belief that it will add to the fighting ability. The preparation is for death in case that should be the result of the conflict. Every Indian wants to look his best when he goes to meet the Great Spirit so the dressing up is done whether in imminent danger in an oncoming battle or a sickness or injury at times of peace.

—WOODEN LEG,
CHEYENNE WARRIOR AND TRIBAL JUDGE,
1858–1940

January 23

There is a dignity about the social intercourse of old Indians which reminds me of a stroll through a winter forest.

—FREDERICK REMINGTON,
NON-NATIVE ARTIST AND SCULPTOR,
1861–1909

In Remembrance

January 23, 1870, at Marias River, Montana, the Baker Massacre, also called "the greatest slaughter of Indians ever made by United States troops," leaves 170 to 215 Indians dead in the snow. They are to be remembered.

January 24

*A people without a history is
like wind on the buffalo grass.*

—TETON SIOUX PROVERB

In Remembrance

Of Ira Hayes (of the Pima tribe),
famous for raising the United States
flag over Iwo Jima with fellow Marines
during World War II. A bronze statue
and postage stamp later commemo-
rated the event. He died on January 24,
1955, at the age of 33. Bob Dylan
immortalized him in the song "The
Ballad of Ira Hayes."

January 25

The Great Spirit . . . made it to always change . . . sunlight to play . . . night to sleep . . . everything good.

—FLYING HAWK,
OGALALA CLAN, 19TH CENTURY

On This Date in
Native American History

January 25, 1968: The Mescalero Apaches were awarded $8.5 million from the United States Indian Claims Commission as compensation for land illegally ceded in the 1800s.

January 26

A Native to Know

Will Rogers, humorist/writer/actor, was born in Indian Territory (Oklahoma) in 1879. Speaking of his Native American heritage, he said, "My folks were Indian. Both my mother and father had Cherokee blood in them. [I was] born and raised in Indian Territory. 'Course we're not the American whose ancestors came over on the *Mayflower*, but they met 'em at the boat when they landed."

Famous for his commentaries and writings, he was known as the "Indian Cowboy" from the Cherokee Nation, and was one of the most popular entertainers of his time. In 1918 he went to Hollywood and starred in many features, becoming such a box office sensation that by 1934 he was voted the most popular male actor in Hollywood. Will Rogers also served as mayor of Beverly Hills, was instrumental in the presidential election of Franklin D. Roosevelt, and even rejected a nomination for governor of Oklahoma. He died in 1935 in a plane crash in Alaska.

January 27

*I'm working for the
Creation. I refuse to take
part in its destruction.*

—Leon Shanandoah,
Iroquois

In Remembrance

Of the Shoshone Indians who
crossed over in the Battle of Bear
River, January 27, 1863.

January 28

Children were encouraged to develop strict discipline and a high regard for sharing. When a girl picked her first berries and dug her first roots, they were given away to an elder so she would share her future success. When a child carried water for the home, an elder would give compliments, pretending to taste meat in water carried by a boy or berries in that of a girl. The child was encouraged not to be lazy and to grow straight like a sapling.

—MOURNING DOVE
(CHRISTINE QUINTASKET), SALISH,
1888–1936

January 29

All things in the world are two. In our minds we are two, good and evil. With our eyes we see two things, things that are fair and things that are ugly . . . We have the right hand that strikes and makes for evil, and we have the left hand full of kindness, near the heart. One foot may lead us to an evil way, the other foot may lead us to a good. So are all things two, all two.

—LETAKOTS-LESA
(GRAY EAGLE CHIEF), PAWNEE,
19TH CENTURY

January 30

I was born in Nature's wide domain!
The trees were all that sheltered my
infant limbs, the blue heavens all that
covered me. I am one of Nature's chil-
dren. I have always admired her.

—GEORGE COPWAY,
OJIBWAY CHIEF, 1818–1863

Did You Know?

Before the Europeans arrived in the
Americas, more than 500 tribes (a
collective group of 22 million people)
inhabited what is now the United States.

January 31

*There is no quiet place in the
white man's cities, no place to
hear the leaves of spring or the
rustle of insect wings . . . the clatter
only seems to insult the ears.*

—CHIEF SEATTLE (SEATHL),
DUWAMISH-SUQUAMISH, 1785–1866

Did You Know?

The following 26 states are named after
Native American words: Alabama, Alaska, Arizona, Arkansas, Connecticut,
Idaho, Illinois, Indiana, Iowa, Kansas,
Kentucky, Massachusetts, Michigan,
Minnesota, Mississippi, Missouri, Nebraska, North Dakota, Ohio, Oklahoma,
South Dakota, Tennessee, Texas, Utah,
Wisconsin, and Wyoming.

FEBRUARY

FEBRUARY NORTHERN
ARAPAHO MOON:
FROST-SPARKLING-IN-THE-SUN MOON

Red Road Ethic 2
Honor Mother Nature

Mother Nature is not *for* us . . . she is *part* of us and we, like everything else that lives and breathes upon her, are her children. Your own direct connection with Mother Earth is to be encouraged daily. Paint her portraits, swim in her waters, tend to her flowers, stroll through her glorious forests, and care for her many children: all plants, people, and animals.

We must live according to her principles and choose not to pollute her body. The alternative is death to our mother—and death to her children.

The Great Spirit is our father, but the Earth is our mother. She nourishes us; that which we put into the ground she returns to us, and healing plants she gives us likewise. If we are wounded, we go to our mother and seek to lay the wounded part against her, to be healed.

—BEDAGI (BIG THUNDER), WABANAKÍ
ALGONQUIN, 1900s

February 1

*The earth is the mother of all
people, and all people should
have equal rights upon it.*

—Chief Joseph
(Hin-mah-too-yah-lat-kekt), Nez Perce,
1840–1904

A Native to Know

Chief Joseph was a major celebrity
during his lifetime. Born in what is
now northeastern Oregon in 1840, he
was the son of one of the first Nez
Perce Christian converts, also named
Joseph, who raised Chief Joseph to
support peace with whites—until the
government betrayed the elder Joseph
and the Nez Perce. Chief Joseph succeeded his father's position in 1871.
After several skirmishes and difficulties
with the U.S. government, he became
an eloquent speaker against injustice
and inequality, and spoke in support
of the freedom of the Native people.

February 2

Lose your temper and you lose a friend; lie and you lose yourself.

—Hopi adage

Did You Know?

A mixture called "kinnikinnick" is typically smoked in peace pipes by Native people. Kinnikinnick is a mixture of various plants and herbs, including sage, white clover, bearberry leaves, and mullein leaves.

February 3

Will we let ourselves be destroyed in our turn without a struggle, give up our homes, our country bequeathed to us by the Great Spirit, the graves of our dead and everything that is dear and sacred to us? I know you will cry with me, "Never! Never!"

—TECUMSEH,
SHAWNEE, 1768–1813

Did You Know?

Traditionally, Native American heritage is handed down from the mother's side, even if both parents are Native American. If only the father is Native American, the Native American lineage is still followed. Some children today, though, follow both parents' lineage.

February 4

All things are the works of the Great Spirit. We should know that He is within all things: the trees, the grasses, the rivers, the mountains, and all the four-legged animals, and the winged peoples; and even more important, we should understand that He is also above all these things and peoples.

—BLACK ELK,
OGLALA SIOUX, 1863–1950

February 5

There was never a better day to die.

—RED HORSE,
LAKOTA, 1876

Did You Know?

The word "Shaman" originated in Siberia, but today some Native tribes and many non-Natives, especially anthropologists, use this term to describe a Native American healer who dwells with the underworld, the supernatural, and the spirits. Individuals who are true shamans will not write a book or make a public appearance about their work, nor will they advertise their practice or speak of it in public. A shaman can only be found by word of mouth, and those who practice ancient customs are rare. They differ from Native healers, who often mix traditional medicine with unconventional methods and act more as a physician to the community.

February 6

What is gained from our inner nature is exact knowledge, which gives us a far-reaching outlook over the earth. The many powers of inner nature are hidden in everyone, and these are identified with Wakan-Tanka.

—BLUE THUNDER,
TETON SIOUX

Did You Know?

Many archaeologists and scholars claim that Native people may have inhabited the Americas as long as 70,000 years prior to non-Natives.

February 7

Then I was standing on the highest mountain of them all, and round about beneath me was the whole hoop of the world. And while I stood there I saw more than I can tell and I understood more than I saw; for I was seeing in a sacred manner the shapes of all things in the spirit, and the shape of all shapes as they must live together like one being . . . And I say the sacred hoop of my people was one of the many hoops that made one circle, wide as daylight and as starlight, and in the center grew one mighty flowering tree to shelter all the children of one mother and one father. And I saw that it was holy . . .

But anywhere is the center of the world.

—BLACK ELK,
OGLALA SIOUX, 1863–1950

February 8

I am not a child. I can think for myself. No man can think for me.

—CHIEF JOSEPH
(HIN-MAH-TOO-YAH-LAT-KEKT), NEZ PERCE,
1840–1904

On This Date in Native American History

February 8, 1887: The Dawes Act, which caused American Indian groups to lose a collected 90 million acres of reservation land, was passed.

February 9

*Yigaquu osaniyu adanvto adadoligi
nigohilvi nasquv utloyasdi nihi
(May the Great Spirit's Blessings
Always Be with You).*

—CHEROKEE ADAGE

A Native to Know

Jay Silverheels was born May 26, 1912,
on the Six Nations Reserve in Ontario,
Canada, to a Mohawk Chief. Silverheels
first worked as a stuntman in Hollywood films, and then as an actor in such
movies as *Key Largo* (1948). In 1949,
Silverheels landed his famous role as
Tonto on the hit television show *The
Lone Ranger,* which ran for eight years.
In 1979, he became the first Native
American awarded a star on Hollywood's Walk of Fame. Silverheels was
inducted into the Hall of Honor of the
First Americans in the Arts in 1998, 18
years after his death.

February 10

*To clothe a man falsely is
only to distress his spirit . . .*

—LUTHER STANDING BEAR,
OGLALA SIOUX, 1868–1937

On This Day in
Native American History

February 10, 1763: France ceded the
North American territory to England in
the Treaty of Paris, ending the French
and Indian War (1754–1763).

February 11

The reason Wakan Tanka does not make two birds . . . or two human beings exactly alike is because each is placed here . . . to be an independent individual to rely on himself.

—OKUTE, 19TH CENTURY

On This Date in Native American History

February 11, 1978: American Indian Movement leader Dennis Banks organized a five-month trek from California to Washington, D.C., to bring awareness to Native American issues. Thousands of people, representing 80 tribes, joined the walk, and they were met in Washington by thousands of supporters lining the city streets and sidewalks.

February 12

Teach your children that the ground beneath their feet is the ashes of our grandfathers. So that they will respect the land, tell your children that the earth is rich with the lives of our kin. Teach your children what we have taught our children—that the earth is our mother. Whatever befalls the earth, befalls the sons of the earth . . . This we know: all things are connected like the blood which unites one family.

—CHIEF SEATTLE (SEATHL),
DUWAMISH-SUQUAMISH, 1785–1866

February 13

You must stop your ears whenever you are asked to sign a treaty selling your home . . . This country holds your father's body. Never sell the bones of your father and your mother.

—OLD CHIEF JOSEPH (TU-EKA-KAS),
NEZ PERCE

On This Date in
Native American History

February 13, 1991: Graham Greene, Oneida, was nominated for Best Supporting Actor by the Academy of Motion Picture Arts and Sciences for his role in the 1990 movie *Dances with Wolves*. He later appeared in *Thunderheart* and *The Green Mile*.

February 14

Great Spirit, you lived first,
and you are older than all need.

—Black Elk,
Oglala Sioux, 1863–1950

On This Date in
Native American History

February 14, 1986: The Smithsonian Institution's Museum of National History agreed to return skeletal remains of American Indians to those tribes with a verifiable lineage. The indigenous people have a burial custom and certain beliefs associated with those who passed on, and holding their ancestral remains is considered sacrilegious.

Red Road Lesson 2
Frybread and Community

Traditionally, frybread is a symbol of intertribal unity and community. It is a staple of powwows and, for many, family meals. The recipes can vary slightly. Here is one that's a personal favorite and is easy to prepare.

> 3 cups flour
> 1 tsp. salt
> 3 tsp. baking powder
> 1 cup milk
> ¼ cup warm water
> Vegetable oil in deep fryer or
>   frying pan

1. Combine flour, salt, and baking powder in a large mixing bowl. Blend ingredients. Slowly stir in milk and knead dough until smooth, adding small amounts of warm water if mixture is too dry. Once dough is ready (when it is stiff and can be molded), cover with a cloth for 15 to 30 minutes.

2. Fill deep fryer or frying pan with oil, and heat until oil is very hot. Pinch off fist-size pieces of the frybread dough and flatten with your hands or with a rolling pin. Fry in the hot oil until golden brown on both sides (approximately 5 minutes). Drain on absorbent paper towels and serve.

Frybread dinner variations:

- Slice in half and serve with your favorite dip
- Use the frybread as the shell of your next taco dinner
- Spread peanut butter, cream cheese, or jelly onto your cooled bread
- Roll warm frybread in sugar for a special treat

Their wishes are our wishes and what we get I hope they will get.

—RUNNING ANTELOPE,
SIOUX, SPEAKING OF FRIENDS AND FAMILY

February 15

The Circle has healing power. In the Circle we are all equal. When in the Circle, no one is in front of you. No one is behind you. No one is above you. No one is below you. The Sacred Circle is designed to create unity. The Hoop of Life is also a circle. On this hoop there is a place for every species, every race, every tree, and every plant. It is this completeness of Life that must be respected in order to bring about health on this planet. To understand each other, as the ripples when a stone is tossed into the waters, the Circle starts small and grows . . . until it fills the whole lake.

—DAVE CHIEF, OGLALA LAKOTA, GRANDSON OF RED DOG/CRAZY HORSE'S BAND

February 16

*The ground on which we
stand is sacred ground.
It is the blood of our ancestors.*

—CHIEF PLENTY COUPS, CROW, 1848–1932

On This Date in
Native American History

February 16, 1835: Congress passed
the Indian Removal Act, initiating the
relocation of thousands of people.

February 17

Let the young men of this nation remember that idleness leads to poverty. Industry is honorable and leads to contentment.

—CHIEF JOHN ROSS, CHEROKEE, 1790–1866

In Remembrance

Of Geronimo, who died on February 17, 1909.

February 18

*Out of the Indian approach to life
there came a great freedom, an
intense and absorbing respect for life,
enriching faith in a Supreme Power,
and principles of truth, honesty, generosity, equity, and brotherhood as a
guide to mundane relations.*

—LUTHER STANDING BEAR,
OGLALA SIOUX, 1868–1937

On This Date in
Native American History

February 18, 1944: In an effort to intro-
duce the beauty of the Native American
culture to the people of New York City,
and to raise funds for Native American
charities, the Indian Confederation of
American Indians staged a colorful
powwow with dancers and participants
representing more than 15 American
Indian tribes.

February 19

*Some of our chiefs make the claim
that the land belongs to us. It is not
what the Great Spirit told me. He told
me that the lands belong to Him, that
no people owns the land; that I was
not to forget to tell this to the white
people when I met them in council.*

—KANAKUK, KICKAPOO,
ADDRESSING GENERAL WILLIAM CLARK, 1827

Did You Know?

A medicine pipe is a sacred tool of
Native tradition used to bring one
closer to the Creator. The smoke acts
as a communication device, bridging
the two worlds.

February 20

*The Kiowa braves have grown up
from childhood, obtaining their
medicine from the earth.*

—SATANTA (WHITE BEAR),
KIOWA, 1830–1878

A Native to Know

Kiowa chief Satanta (Set'-tain-te) dev-
oted himself to the preservation of the
Kiowa way of life. He was an eloquent
speaker whom the whites called the
Orator of the Plains.

February 21

*If I have these and kept back the best
no one would believe I was in earnest.
I must give something that I really
value to show that my whole being
goes with the lesser gifts; therefore
I promise to give my body.*

—CHASED-BY-BEARS,
SANTEE-YANKTONAI SIOUX, 1843–1915

In Remembrance

Of Walt Bresette, Red Cliff Chippewa, who died February 21, 1999, at the age of 51.

Bresette cofounded the Midwest Treaty Network and cowrote the book, *Walleye Warriors: An Effective Alliance Against Racism and for the Earth.*

February 22

*Do right always. It will give
you satisfaction in life.*

—WOVOKA (JACK WILSON),
PAIUTE SPIRITUAL LEADER, 1889

A Native to Know

Wovoka woke the Native nations when
he originated the Ghost Dance Religion
in 1889. A prophet and spiritual leader,
Wovoka believed there would one day
be a time when all Indian people—
those living and those who had died—
would be reunited. In early 1890, the
Ghost Dance Religion spread to many
tribes throughout the West. Also in 1890,
the Office of Indian Affairs outlawed the
religion, arresting those who participated. After the death of Sitting Bull
(arrested for suspicion of being a Ghost
Dance leader), Big Foot and his band
traveled to Wounded Knee where he
and 300 other men, women, and children were killed. Despite the pro-
hibitory law, practice of the Ghost
Dance continued in secret until 1978.

February 23

O ye people, be ye healed; Life anew
I bring unto ye. O ye people, be ye
healed; Life anew I bring unto ye.
Through the Father and all Do I thus.
Life anew I bring unto ye.

—GOOD EAGLE (WANBLI-WASTE),
DAKOTA SIOUX, LATE 19TH CENTURY

In Remembrance

Of Quanah Parker, known as the last free chief of the Comanche, who crossed over today in 1911. He never lost a battle to white troops and fought passionately for the rights of his people.

February 24

Whatever the gains,
whatever the loss, they are yours.

—Five Wounds,
Nez Perce

A Native to Know

Novelist and poet N. Scott Momaday, born 1934, is considered one of the premier writers in the United States today. His books have achieved much literary success, and he won a Pulitzer Prize for his 1969 novel, *House Made of Dawn*. Momaday is a Kiowa and was raised on various Native reservations, and his writings reflect his love of his people, his culture, and his land. A graduate of Stanford University (with both a master's and doctoral degree), he created the Indian literature program at the University of California, in Berkeley.

February 25

We do not want riches.
We want peace and love.

—RED CLOUD (MAKHPIYA-LUTA),
OGLALA SIOUX, 1870

In Remembrance

Of those who died on February 25, 1643, in what is known as "The Slaughter of the Innocents." Considered one of the worst Native American slaughters in United States history, the massacre was the result of an order given by the director-general of New Netherlands to rid his territory of Indians. Several bands of tribes were exterminated and thousands of women, men, and children died.

February 26

The old Lakota was wise. He knew that man's heart away from nature becomes hard.

—LUTHER STANDING BEAR,
OGLALA SIOUX, 1868–1937

Did You Know?

The largest reservation in the United States is the Navajo Indian Reservation (Utah, New Mexico, and Arizona) with nearly 3.5 million acres of land.

February 27

*We are contented to
let things remain as the
Great Spirit made them.*

—CHIEF JOSEPH
(HIN-MAH-TOO-YAH-LAT-KEKT),
NEZ PERCE, 1840–1904

On This Date in
Native American History

February 27, 1973: Wounded
Knee II erupted in South
Dakota.

February 28

Make everything straight and strong.

—DRAGGING CANOE,
CHICKAMAUGA TSALAGI

Did You Know?

There are many well-known Hollywood celebrities with claims to Native American lineage.

A few examples include A. Martinez, Brian Austin Green, Burt Reynolds, Carmen Electra, Cher, Chuck Norris, Della Reese, Elvis Presley, Heather Locklear, Hunter Tylo, James Earl Jones, James Garner, Johnny Cash, Johnny Depp, Jon Leguizamo, Kim Basinger, Bill Maher, Stephanie Kramer, Tommy Lee Jones, and Val Kilmer.

MARCH

MARCH CHEROKEE MOON:
"ANVHYI" OR STRAWBERRY MOON

*Spring—known as Sigun in Cree—
is upon us.*

Red Road Ethic 3
Search for Yourself, by Yourself

Do not allow others to make your path for you. It is *your* road and yours alone. Others may walk it *with* you, but no one can walk it *for* you. Accept yourself and your actions. Own your thoughts. Speak up when wrong, and apologize. Know your path at all times. To do this you must know yourself inside and out, accept your gifts as well as your shortcomings, and grow each day with honesty, integrity, compassion, faith, and brotherhood.

I have made myself what I am.

—TECUMSEH,
SHAWNEE, 1768–1813

March 1

*Sometimes dreams are
wiser than waking*

—Black Elk,
Oglala Sioux, 1863–1950

Did You Know?

The first Native American newspaper,
published in 1828, was the *Cherokee
Phoenix*.

March 2

When the Earth is sick, the animals will begin to disappear, when that happens, The Warriors of the Rainbow will come to save them.

—CHIEF SEATTLE (SEATHL),
DUWAMISH-SUQUAMISH, 1785–1866

Did You Know?

Annie Dodge Wauneka, Navajo, received the Presidential Medal of Freedom Award in 1963 from President John F. Kennedy. The medal, granted to those who make outstanding contributions to peace, is the country's highest peacetime honor.

March 3

Let us look forward to the pleasing landscape of the future.

—CHIEF JOHN ROSS,
CHEROKEE, 1790–1866

A Native to Know

Simon Ortiz, Pueblo, won the Pushcart Prize for Poetry in 1981 for his collection entitled *From Sand Creek*. Ortiz holds a master's degree of fine arts and taught writing and literature at a number of colleges and universities.

March 4

The path of glory is rough and many gloomy hours obscure it. May the Great Spirit shed light on yours.

—BLACK HAWK,
SAUK, 1767–1838

Did You Know?

To many Native Americans, the term "bad medicine" means having a streak of bad luck, or that the spirits are working against them.

March 5

Our land is everything to us . . .
I will tell you one of the things we
remember on our land. We
remember that our grandfathers
paid for it—with their lives.

—WOODEN LEG,
CHEYENNE WARRIOR AND TRIBAL JUDGE,
1858–1940

Did You Know?

Through the centuries—and even today—there have been many female chieftains of various Native American tribal communities.

March 6

My friend, I am going to tell you the story of my life, as you wish; and if it were only the story of my life I think I would not tell it; for what is one man that he should make much of his winters, even when they bend him like a heavy snow? So many other men have lived and shall live that story, to be grass upon the hills.

—Black Elk,
Oglala Sioux, 1863–1950

A Native to Know

Black Elk was born in 1863 on the Little Powder River. When he was nine years old he received a vision that gave him a "special power," a power instrumental in his later becoming a prominent member of his tribe. A religious medicine man, he traveled the world and spoke to many about his beliefs and spirituality. In 1950, on the Pine Ridge Reservation, he crossed over.

March 7

There is one God looking down on us all. We are all children of one God. God is listening to me. The sun, the darkness, the winds, are all listening to what we now say.

—GOYATHLAY (GERONIMO),
APACHE MEDICINE MAN AND WAR CHIEF,
1829–1909

On This Date in
Native American History

March 7, 1934: Douglas Joseph Cardinal, Blackfoot, was born in Alberta, Canada. He is well known as a celebrated architect, and was commissioned in 1983 to design the Canadian Museum of Civilization building—a project worth over $90 million. In 1985 he was the chief architect of the National Museum of the American Indians project.

March 8

The soil you see is not ordinary soil—it is the dust of the blood, the flesh, and bones of our ancestors . . . You will have to dig through the surface before you can find nature's earth, as the upper portion is Crow. The land, as it is, is my blood and my dead; it is consecrated.

—SHES-HIS,
RENO CROW, LATE 19TH CENTURY

March 9

We do not walk alone.
Great Being walks beside us.
Know this and be grateful.

—Polingaysi Qoyawayma,
Hopi, born 1892

In Remembrance

Of the 90 innocent Christian Delaware
Indians killed on March 9, 1782, in
Gnadenhutten, Ohio.

March 10

*Civilized people depend too much
on man-made printed pages.
I turn to the Great Spirit's book
which is the whole of his creation.*

—TATANGA MANI, 1871–1967

On This Date in
Native American History

March 10, 1861: Famed Mohawk poet E.
Pauline Johnson was born to an English
mother and a Mohawk father in Ontario
at the Six Nations Reserve. She later
published many works of poetry and
novels including *The White Wampum*
(1895) and *Canadian Born* (1903). She
toured England, North America, and
Canada reading her poetry in front of
live audiences, and became highly
acclaimed for her writing.

March 11

*I never want to leave this country;
all my relatives are lying here in
the ground, and when I fall to pieces
I am going to fall to pieces here.*

—WOLF NECKLACE,
PALOUSE

Did You Know?

A coup stick is a device used by Native
Americans to strike an enemy, and it
was a great achievement to strike the
enemy without wounding them or without their knowledge of the presence of
the person couping.

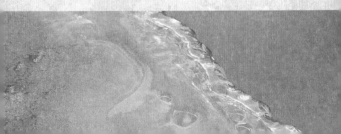

March 12

As a child I understood how to give;
I have forgotten this grace
since I became civilized.

—OHIYESA (CHARLES EASTMAN),
SANTEE SIOUX, 1858–1939

On This Date in
Native American History

March 12, 1880: Judge Elmer Dundy resolved that Native Americans are indeed "persons within the meaning of the law" and have the same rights as any other person. Until then, it was debated whether an Indian was a real person or an animal.

March 13

*To fight is to forget ourselves
as Indians in the world.*

—Dr. Carlos Montezuma,
Yavapai

A Native to Know

Montezuma (II) is probably the most familiar figure in Aztec history. He led his people during the time of the Spanish conquest and was held hostage by Hernan Cortés for ransom until the 1520 Aztec revolt. Montezuma was stoned while talking to his people and died three days later.

March 14

*Each man is good in His sight. It is
not necessary for eagles to be crows.*

—HUNKESNI (SITTING BULL),
HUNKPAPA SIOUX, 1831–1890

Did You Know?

The drum is one of the most important
instruments used by the Native people.
Often referred to as the "heartbeat of the
people," the drum keeps order through
rhythm, especially when dancing.

Red Road Lesson 3
The Many Names
of the Great Spirit

The Great Spirit is the name given to the life force radiating from all creation. This energy is called many things by many different people: the Creator, A'wonawil'onas (Zuni), Wankan-Tankan (Sioux), God, Tirawa (Pawnee), Great Mystery, and Grandfather.

We may quarrel with men about things on Earth, but we never quarrel about the Great Spirit.

—CHIEF JOSEPH
(HIN-MAH-TOO-YAH-LAT-KEKT), NEZ PERCE,
1840–1904

March 15

I have noticed in my life that all men have a liking for some special animal, tree, plant, or spot of earth. If men would pay more attention for these preferences and seek what is best to do in order to make themselves worthy of that toward which they are so attracted, they might have dreams which would purify their lives. Let a man decide upon his favorite animal and make a study of it, learning its innocent ways. Let him learn to understand its sounds and motions. The animals want to communicate with man, but Wakan Tanka does not intend they shall do so directly—man must do the greater part in securing an understanding.

—BRAVE BUFFALO,
TETON SIOUX, LATE 19TH CENTURY

March 16

*When we lift our hands we signify
our dependence on the Great Spirit.*

—Blackfoot,
Mountain Crow leader

A Native to Know

Notah Begay III, born in New Mexico, 1972, is the first Native American Indian to join the PGA Tour. Begay is Navajo, San Felipe, and Isleta—all tribes from the southwestern United States. Former teammate Tiger Woods said Begay is "happy to represent the Native American people, and in some regards, be a role model."

March 17

When we Indians kill meat, we eat it all up. When we dig roots, we make little holes. When we build houses, we make little holes. When we burn grass for grasshoppers, we don't ruin things. We shake down acorns and pine nuts. We don't chop down the trees. We only use dead wood. But the White people plow up the ground, pull down the trees, kill everything . . . the White people pay no attention . . . How can the spirit of the earth like the White man? . . . everywhere the White man has touched it, it is sore.

—WINTU WOMAN,
19TH CENTURY

March 18

*I have always taught you
that a liar is not worthy of
being considered a man . . .*

—STUNG ARM

Did You Know?

The portrait on the U.S. buffalo
nickels, sculpted in 1911, is said to
be the composite of three Native
Americans: Iron Tail, Big Tree, and
Two Moons.

March 19

I am poor and naked but I am the chief of a nation. We do not want riches but we do want to train our children right. Riches would do us no good. We could not take them with us to the other world. We do not want riches. We want peace and love.

—RED CLOUD (MAKHPIYA-LUTA),
OGLALA SIOUX CHIEF, 1822–1909

On This Date in
Native American History

March 19, 1827: Cherokee author, journalist, and activist John Rillin Ridge was born.

March 20

*O Great Spirit, help me never
judge another until I have walked
two weeks in his moccasins.*

—EDWIN LAUGHING FOX

Did You Know?

In 1774, Thomas Paine studied the
Iroquois Confederacy, culture, and language in order to further his education
in democratic government.

March 21

The Kiowa braves have grown up from childhood, obtaining their medicine from the earth.

—SATANK,
KIOWA, C. 1810–1871

Did You Know?

There are many common foods that are of Native American origin. A few are pumpkin, zucchini, squash, sweet potatoes, peanuts, maple syrup, and hot chocolate.

March 22

Our bare feet are conscious of the sympathetic touch of our ancestors as we walk over this Earth.

—Chief Seattle (Seathl),
Duwamish-Suquamish, 1785–1866

Did You Know?

A Shaman is generally a person who uses healing practices to treat and prevent illnesses associated with negative spirits, while medicine men and medicine women treat illnesses caused by both natural and supernatural forces.

March 23

*We do not take up the
warpath without a just cause
and honest purpose.*

—PUSHMATAHA,
CHOCTAW TRIBAL LEADER, 1764–1824

A Native to Know

Pushmataha was a Choctaw chief who
kept peace with the U.S. government,
even when it meant siding against
such influential men as Tecumseh. His
services to the government earned him
the rank of U.S. brigadier general, and
when he died in 1824, he was buried
with full U.S. military honors.

March 24

*Misfortunes do not flourish
particularly in our path.
They grow everywhere.*

—Black Elk,
Oglala Sioux, 1863–1950

Did You Know?

Several games were played by Native
people prior to 1492, including bad-
minton, field hockey, cat's cradle,
darts, lacrosse, and spinning tops.

March 25

While living I want to live well. I know I have to die sometime, but even if the heavens were to fall on me, I want to do what is right. I think I am a good man . . . There is one God looking down on us all. We are all children of the one God. God is listening to me. The sun, the darkness, the winds, are all listening to what we now say.

—GOYATHLAY (GERONIMO),
APACHE MEDICINE MAN AND WAR CHIEF,
TO GENERAL GEORGE CROOK DURING
A PEACE CONFERENCE, MARCH 25, 1886

March 26

*Neither anger nor fear shall
find lodging in your mind.*

—DEKANAWIDAH,
IROQUOIS, C. 1300

On This Date in
Native American History

March 26, 1839: The Trail of Tears
ended.

March 27

If we could have spared more,
we would have given more . . .

—CANASSATEGO,
ONONDAGA

On This Date in
Native American History

March 27, 1973: At the Academy Awards presentation, Marlon Brando protested the mistreatment of American Indians.

March 28

The Great Spirit will not punish us for what we do not know.

—RED JACKET (SAGOYEWATHA),
SENECA, C. 1752–1830

Did You Know?

The totem pole has been a part of the Alaskan tribes' history for centuries. Carved from a column of wood, the pole depicts various animal and mythological symbols important to the individual, family, and/or tribe.

March 29

To the Indian, words that are true sink deep into his heart where they remain; he never forgets them.

—FOUR GUNS

Did You Know?

In 1744 Benjamin Franklin sought the advice of Chief Canassatego on how to unite the American colonies into one confederacy.

March 30

*Why don't you talk and go
straight and all will be well?*

—Black Kettle,
Southern Cheyenne chief

A Native to Know

There are few personal details
known about Black Kettle, a
Southern Cheyenne chief, but
what is known about him is
legendary. He was an eloquent
speaker, a dedicated leader, and
a consistent champion of his
people.

March 31

Your feet shall be as swift as forked lightning; your arm shall be as the thunderbolt, and your soul fearless.

—Methoataske

Did You Know?

A medicine bag, or medicine bundle, is carried by many Native people to hold sacred objects—such as stones, animal talons, totem, sacred herbs, or other prized possessions. It is worn on their body and kept close to them at all times. These items protect the individual and are used during sacred ceremonies or events. A "totem" is an object (animal, plant, etc.) that an individual is intimately related to. The person has a bond with this item, and uses it for prayer or to draw strength from during times of need.

THE EASTERN
JOURNEY OF SPRING

Yellow is the color of Mother Earth's sunsets, and the color of spring. The east is the direction of a new day, of new beginnings, and of first light. Spring is the perfect time to start new projects, raise your own vegetables and herbs, and to overcome challenges such as kicking bad habits.

Direction: East
Season: Spring
Color: Yellow

*My heart is filled with joy, when
I see you here, as the brook fills
with water when the snows melt in
the spring, and I feel glad, as the
ponies are when the fresh grass starts
in the beginning of the year.*

—TEN BEARS,
YAMPARIKA COMANCHE

APRIL

APRIL MOHAWK MOON:
ONERAHTOKHA: THE BUDDING TIME

Red Road Ethic 4
Community Code of Conduct

Treat the guests in your home with much consideration. Serve them the best food, give them the best bed, and treat them with respect. Honor the thoughts, wishes, and words of others. Never interrupt another or mock or mimic them. Allow each person the right to freedom of opinion. Respect that opinion. Never speak ill of others. As you travel along life's road never harm anyone, nor cause anyone to feel sad. On the contrary, if at any time you can make a person happy, do so.

Even as you desire good treatment, so render it.

—HANDSOME LAKE,
SENECA, C. 1735–1815

April 1

Naturally the Indian has many noble qualities. He is the very embodiment of courage. Indeed, at times he seems insensible to fear. If he is cruel and revengeful, it is because he is outlawed and his companion is the wild beast.

—N. G. TAYLOR,
U.S. COMMISSIONER, 1868

A Native to Know

Norval Morrisseau (Copper Thunderbird) was born on March 14, 1932, on Sand Point Ojibway Reserve in Ontario. An accomplished artist, he founded an art school in Canada, the Woodland School, has exhibited more than 40 one-man shows (many in France), received the prestigious Order of Canada Medal in 1978, and was elected to the Royal Canadian Academy of the Arts. In 1989 he became the only Canadian painter asked to exhibit in the Paris French Revolution Bicentennial.

April 2

*You must speak straight so
that your words may go as
sunlight to our hearts.*

—COCHISE,
CHIRICAHUA APACHE TRIBAL LEADER,
1812–1874

A Native to Know

Cochise was chief of the Chiricahua
Apache and known for his intelligence
and strategic strength. U.S. Cavalry soldiers referred to him as "The Serpent."

April 3

That hand is not the color of your hand, but if I pierce it I shall feel pain. The blood that will follow from mine will be the same color as yours. The Great Spirit made us both.

—LUTHER STANDING BEAR,
OGLALA SIOUX, 1868–1937

On This Date in
Native American History

April 3, 1994: In New Mexico, artist Charlene Teters closed her controversial exhibit "It Was Only an Indian: Native American Stereotypes."

April 4

My forefathers were warriors.
Their son is a warrior. From
them I take my existence, from
my tribe I take nothing. I am
the maker of my own fortune.

—TECUMSEH,
SHAWNEE, 1768–1813

On This Date in
Native American History

April 4, 1991: According to the U.S. census, 1,959,234 American Indians live in the United States.

April 5

*Men must be born
and reborn to belong.*

—LUTHER STANDING BEAR,
OGLALA SIOUX, 1868–1937

A Native to Know

Poet and novelist Sherman Alexie, born
in 1966 and brought up on a Spokane
Indian Reservation, has won several
awards for his writing, including the
National Endowment for the Arts Poetry
Fellowship in 1992. With more than 200
published poems and stories, he is best
known for the book *The Lone Ranger
and Tonto Fistfight in Heaven* (1993).

April 6

My words make haste to reach your ears, harken to them.

—GARANGULA,
ONONDAGA, 1684

Did You Know?

To the Haudenosaunee, the symbol of arrows bundled together signifies unity and brotherhood among Native nations.

April 7

There is no death . . .
Only a change of worlds.

—CHIEF SEATTLE (SEATHL),
DUWAMISH-SUQUAMISH, 1785–1866

A Native to Know

Cory Witherill (born 1971), Navajo, holds the distinction of being the most successful Native American race car driver in history. Witherill has raced several times in the PPG Dayton Indy Lights Championship, and in 2001 raced his first Indianapolis 500.

April 8

*Stand fast and remain united
and all will soon be well.*

—CHIEF JOHN ROSS,
CHEROKEE, 1790–1866

Did You Know?

There are hundreds of words in the American English language borrowed from or influenced by indigenous languages. Here are just a few: chocolate, tomato, llama, caribou, moose, persimmon, opossum, raccoon, muskrat, skunk, pecan, puma, caucus, kayak, toboggan, hickory, squash, hooch, chipmunk, woodchuck, and bayou.

April 9

Hoka hey! Follow me! Follow me!
Today is a good day to fight,
today is a good day to die!

—CRAZY HORSE,
OGLALA-BRULÉ SIOUX, JUNE 1876

A Native to Know

Crazy Horse, Oglala-Brulé Sioux, was born east of the sacred Black Hills in 1842. He later became the war leader of an Oglala subgroup, the Teton Sioux, and was involved in several skirmishes including the Battle of the Little Bighorn. He surrendered in 1877 and was then killed.

April 10

*The Earth and myself
are of one mind.*

—Chief Joseph
(Hin-mah-too-yah-lat-kekt), Nez
Perce, 1840–1904

Did You Know?

A potlatch is a lavish ceremonial feast of the Northwest Coast tribal communities where extravagant gifts are exchanged between host and attendees.

April 11

Convince the world by your character that Indians are not as they have been shown.

—CHIEF JOHN ROSS,
CHEROKEE, 1790–1866

On This Date in
Native American History

April 11, 1968: The American Indian Civil Rights Act was passed by the U.S. Congress.

April 12

*Never has the earth been so lovely
nor the sun so bright, as today . . .*

—Nikinapi

A Native to Know

Sequoyah (1770–1843), Cherokee, developed a syllabary for the Cherokee language and opened many new doors for his fellow people. It took Sequoyah 12 years to finish his work, and he will be remembered as one of the only people in world history to create an entire syllabary on his own.

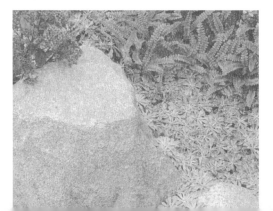

April 13

Savages we call them, because their manners differ from ours, which we think the perfection of civility; they think the same of theirs. Perhaps, if we could examine the manners of different nations with impartiality, we should find no people so rude as to be without any rules of politeness; nor any so polite, as not to have some remains of rudeness . . . The politeness of these savages in conversation is indeed carried to excess, since it does not permit them to contradict, or deny the truth of what is asserted in their presence. By this means they indeed avoid disputes, but then it becomes difficult to know their minds, or what impression you make upon them. The missionaries who have attempted to convert them to Christianity, all complain of this as one of the great difficulties of their mission. The Indians hear with patience the truths of the Gospel explained to them, and give their usual tokens of assent and approbation; you would think they were convinced. No such matter. It is mere civility.

—BENJAMIN FRANKLIN, 1783

April 14

In all your official acts, self-interest shall be cast aside. You shall look and listen to the welfare of the whole people and have always in view, not only the present but the coming generations— the unborn of the future Nation.

—DEKAWIDAH,
CHEROKEE, 1720

Red Road Lesson 4
The Tree of Life

The Tree of Life represents all that is life, encompassing all that exists upon the planet. When we walk the Red Road, our journey ends under the protection of this Tree. It causes the rhythm of the world to continue year after year, and with each cycle, fruit nourishes those who stand under her boughs. The roots dig deep into history. Those dedicated to this energy know the value of all beings, tend to Mother Earth, and live an honorable life in honor of the spirit of the ancient Tree.

The white man is too far removed from America's formative processes. The roots of the tree of his life have not yet grasped the rock and soil. . . . But for the Indian, the spirit of the land is still vested . . . When the Indian has forgotten the music of his forefathers, when the sound of the tom-tom is no more, when the memory of his heroes is no longer told in story . . . he will be dead.

—LUTHER STANDING BEAR,
OGLALA SIOUX CHIEF, 1905–1939

April 15

. . . for the Indian the spirit of the land is still vested; it will be until other men are able to divine and meet its rhythm.

—LUTHER STANDING BEAR,
OGLALA SIOUX, 1868–1937

Did You Know?

Helen Hunt Jackson (1830–1885) was a novelist whose controversial work included a novel exploring the U.S. government's mistreatment of Native Americans. *A Century of Dishonor* detailed the government's role in violating treaties and violating basic human rights. Published in 1881, her revolutionary book created quite a sensation and even today is still in print.

April 16

Listen or your tongue
will keep you deaf.

—NATIVE AMERICAN PROVERB

Did You Know?

Lacrosse is a game with Native American origins, though the actual name stems from a French priest who, in 1705, saw Algonquin Indians playing the sport and thought the webbed sticks resembled a bishop's cross. The sticks and the game were eventually renamed lacrosse.

April 17

*Teach us the road to travel,
and we will not
depart from it forever.*

—SATANK,
KIOWA, C. 1810–1871

On This Date in
Native American History

April 17, 1680: Catherine, Mohawk,
died. She was the first American
Indian to become a Catholic nun.

April 18

You must not hurt anybody or do harm to anyone. You must not fight but do right always.

—WOVOKA (JACK WILSON), PAIUTE SPIRITUAL LEADER, C. 1856–1932

A Native to Know

One of the most well known Native leaders of Ohio is Chief Tarhe (the Crane). In 1794 the Wyandot leader was involved in the Battle of Fallen Timbers and fought for the rights and land of his people. In the War of 1812, at the age of 70, Tarhe led his warriors into battle. He was known by whites and Indians alike as a noble man.

April 19

The monitor within my breasts has taught me the will of the Great Spirit . . .

—SENACHWINE,
POTAWATOMI

On This Date in
Native American History

April 19, 1907: Canadian long-distance runner Tom Longboat, Onondaga, won the Boston Marathon.

April 20

. . . I have seen that in any great undertaking it is not enough for a man to depend simply upon himself.

—Lone Man (Isna-la-wica), Teton Sioux, late 19th century

Did You Know?

Nevada was first known as the Washoe Territory, named after the Washoe Indians.

April 21

*Take only memories,
leave nothing but footprints.*

—CHIEF SEATTLE (SEATHL),
DUWAMISH-SUQUAMISH, 1785–1866

A Native to Know

Maria Martinez is considered one of the greatest American Indian potters of the 20th century. Born in 1886, she worked with archaeologists in 1907 and copied work of pottery found at excavations. She is most famous for her black-on-white pottery, a tradition passed to her daughter.

April 22

It is important to understand that there are many different ways of seeing the world and expressing the wisdom of Native belief . . . No one voice speaks for all voices . . .

—JOSEPH BRUCHAC,
FROM HIS BOOK *NATIVE WISDOM*

Did You Know?

Robbie Robertson, best known for being a member of the 1970s group The Band, connected with his Native American roots after the 1994 television documentary *Music for the Native Americans.* His songs, for the documentary, a mix of rock, cutting-edge sounds, and Native chants and myths, are well received both by Native people and non-Natives.

April 23

Abuse no one and no living thing, for abuse turns the wise ones to fools and robs the spirit of its vision. When it comes your time to die, be not like those whose hearts are filled with fear of death, so that when their time comes they weep and pray for a little more time to live their lives over again in a different way. Sing your death song and die like a hero going home.

—TECUMSEH,
SHAWNEE, 1768–1813

April 24

I beg you now to believe this, all miserable as we seem in your eyes, we consider ourselves nevertheless much happier than thou, in that we are very content with the little that we have . . . Thou deceivest thyselves greatly if thou thinkest to persuade us that thy country is better than ours.

—GASPESIAN CHIEF, 1676

Did You Know?

The term "Eskimo"—which means "the eater of raw flesh"—is considered derogatory by many Alaskan Natives. The preferred term is "Inuit."

April 25

A child believes that only the action of someone who is unfriendly can cause pain.

—CHASED-BY-BEARS,
SANTEE-YANKTONAI SIOUX, 1843–1915

Did You Know?

Traditional Hopi have a specific procedure for naming their children. The first 20 days following birth, mother and child stay in an isolated room hidden from the sun. After the 20 days, the child is presented to the sun to be blessed and is given several names. One name is the childhood name; other names will be decided later as the child grows, changes, and evolves.

April 26

When you arise in the morning,
give thanks for the morning light,
for your life and strength. Give
thanks for your food and the joy of
living. If you see no reason for giving
thanks, the fault lies in yourself.

—TECUMSEH,
SHAWNEE, 1768–1813

April 27

*Take the best of the white man's road,
pick it up and take it with you. That
which is bad leave alone, cast it away.
Take the best of the old Indian ways—
always keep them. They have been
proven for thousands of years. Do not
let them die.*

—ATTRIBUTED TO HUNKESNI (SITTING BULL),
HUNKPAPA SIOUX, 1831–1890

April 28

The American Indian is of the soil, whether it be the region of forests, plains, pueblos, or mesas. He fits into the landscape, for the hand that fashioned the continent also fashioned the man for his surroundings. He once grew as naturally as the wild sunflowers, he belongs just as the buffalo belonged . . .

—LUTHER STANDING BEAR,
OGLALA SIOUX, 1868–1937

April 29

They could not capture me except under a white flag. They cannot hold me except with a chain.

—OSCEOLA, SEMINOLE,
MADE PRISONER OF WAR WHILE UNDER A FLAG OF TRUCE. HE DIED IN HIS PRISON CELL IN 1838.

Did You Know?

Indigenous peoples have been making baskets for thousands of years out of grasses, reeds, and sticks. And today, basketmaking is still a strong art practiced by many tribes, including the Hopi, Ute, and Shoshone.

April 30

We concealed nothing.
We came not secretly nor in the night.
We came in open day.

—MANGAS COLORADAS,
APACHE, 1797–1863

In Remembrance

Of those 144 defenseless Aravaipa Apache Indians who were murdered by an angry mob on April 30, 1871, at Camp Grant.

Red Road Ethic 5
Banish Fear from Your Life

Fear stunts your soul and limits the amount of road needed to travel to reach the Tree of Life, and to know the Great Spirit. Fear is nonbeneficial and leads to an unbalanced mind, body, and spirit. To banish fear you must know your path and trust yourself— and the world around you. With trust comes confidence. Self-confidence banishes fear.

I fear no man,
and I depend on the Great Spirit.

—KONDIARONK,
HURON, LATE 17TH CENTURY

MAY

MAY WINNEBAGO MOON:
HOEING CORN MOON

May 1

Together the two paths form a north-south road, the good Red Road. This is your spiritual path, the one where you will be happiest.

—MEDICINE HAWK,
COUNCIL CHIEF OF THE
SHADOWLIGHT MEDICINE CLAN

Did You Know?

In all Native American languages still spoken today, there is no word for "religion." Native people do not consider their beliefs one of religion. There is no fixed dogma or a list of written rules. There is only an understanding that one is to seek one's own path and live right with nature and right with the world.

May 2

*We like our religion,
and do not want another.*

—RED JACKET (SAGOYEWATHA),
SENECA, 1811

Did You Know?

There is often a set protocol for how to search for wild plants for medicinal uses.
Often the rules include showing respect and thanking the plant for its sacrifice.

May 3

We shall live as brothers as long as sun and moon shine in the sky. We have a broad path to walk. If the Indian sleep and the Yengeesman come, he pass and do not harm to the Indian. If Yengeesman sleep in path, the Indian pass and do him no harm. Indian say, "He's Yengees; he loves sleep."

—TAMMANY,
DELAWARE CHIEF, 1682

May 4

*Given the proper incentive,
no mountain, it seems, is too
high to climb, no current too swift
to swim, if one is a Cherokee.*

—GRACE STEELE WOODWARD,
AUTHOR

On This Date in
Native American History

May 4, 1999: Sacagawea and her infant child were chosen to appear on the new golden United States dollar coin.

May 5

We don't have gold temples in this lake, but we have a sign of a living God to whom we pray—the living trees, the evergreen and spruce and the beautiful flowers and the beautiful rocks and the lake itself . . . We are taking that water to give us strength so we can gain in knowledge and wisdom . . . That is the reason this Blue Lake is so important to us.

—THE 1961 ASSOCIATION ON
AMERICAN INDIAN AFFAIRS TAOS SPOKESMAN

May 6

*Where I am, I build my house;
and where I build my house,
all things come to it.*

—OSAGE INDIAN PROVERB

Did You Know?

Native American people were forbidden to legally practice the Ghost Dance until 1978.

May 7

*When we use water in the sweat lodge
we should think of Wakan-Tanka who
is always flowing, giving His power
and life to everything; we should even
be as water which is lower than all
things, yet stronger than the rocks.*

—BLACK ELK,
OGLALA SIOUX, 1863–1950

May 8

It has come to me through the bushes that you are not yet all united; take time and become united . . .

—Big Bear

Did You Know?

The terms "Grandfather" and "Grandmother" are used to show respect to an elder, whether or not they are related by blood.

May 9

*Just what Power is I cannot explain,
for it is beyond my comprehension.
Those who seek it go alone that they
may be tested for worthiness. It is a
gift to be bestowed not only for
virtue but for prayer and courage.*

—VICTORIO,
MIMBRES APACHE, 1820–1880

Did You Know?

In Native American tradition, there are
two basic categories of songs: those
written by people, and songs given to
an individual through visions or dreams.

May 10

Is there not something worthy of per-petuation in our Indian spirit of democracy, where Earth, our mother, was free to all, and no one sought to impoverish or enslave his neighbor?

—OHIYESA (CHARLES EASTMAN),
SANTEE SIOUX, 1858–1939

A Native to Know

Ohiyesa, of the Eastern Woodland Santee Sioux, was born in 1858 and raised traditionally with his Woodland Sioux grandmother in southwestern Minnesota until he was 15. He was later educated at Dartmouth and then Boston University Medical School, where he delivered the graduation address to his fellow classmates. Ohiyesa is well known today for his writing, storytelling, essays, and lectures.

May 11

If the Great Spirit had desired me to be a white man he would have made me so in the first place. He put in your heart certain wishes and plans, in my heart he put other and different desires . . . Now we are poor but we are free. No white man controls our footsteps. If we must die we die defending our rights.

—HUNKESNI (SITTING BULL),
HUNKPAPA SIOUX, 1831–1890

May 12

We work as hard as you do.
Did you ever try
skinning a buffalo?

—OURAY, UNCOMPAHGRE UTE CHIEF,
UPSET WHEN ACCUSED OF BEING LAZY

Did You Know?

Native Americans have created beads out of copper, stone, bones, shells, clay, and glass. Bead artistry is continued by thousands of Native artisans, who create work both traditional and contemporary.

May 13

*Let us look forward to the
pleasing landscape of the future.*

—Chief John Ross,
Cherokee, 1790–1866

On This Date in
Native American History

May 13, 1916: "Indian Day" was recognized by the Society of American
Indians (a group of non-Native supporters), who wished to recognize the
plight of the Native people and to
honor their legacy.

May 14

Training began with children who were taught to sit still and enjoy it. They were taught to use their organs of smell, to look when there was apparently nothing to see, and to listen intently when all seemingly was quiet. A child that cannot sit still is a half-developed child.

—LUTHER STANDING BEAR,
OGLALA SIOUX, 1868–1937

Did You Know?

Activist and artist Charlene Teters is called the "Rosa Parks" of the American Indians for her controversial work and exhibits (such as the exhibit "It Was Only an Indian"), which speak out against stereotyping Native people in the media, for commercial purposes, and in sports mascots. Her activism was made into a documentary entitled *In Whose Honor*. She is known as one of today's most respected Native leaders.

Red Road Lesson 5
The Medicine Wheel

The Medicine Wheel is the symbol of all creation. This ancient emblem represents all of life's forces. The Medicine Wheel explains our existence It tells what is true and what is needed to live.

The Medicine Wheel, is divided into four parts. Those four parts represent the whole of the person, the whole of the Creator, or the whole of the universe. A Medicine Wheel representing life would include birth/death, childhood, adulthood, and old age.

The Wheel may symbolize "self"—spiritual, emotional, physical, and mental. If a person lacks one aspect of the wheel, or one section is sick or lagging, the Medicine Wheel will remain unbalanced and the self will not be whole. Once the area is mended, the self can focus on its path.

Humankind has not woven the web of life. We are but one thread within it. Whatever we do to the web, we do to ourselves. All things are bound together.

—CHIEF SEATTLE (SEATHL),
DUWAMISH-SUQUAMISH, 1785–1866

May 15

The chastisement of God is worse than any physical pain or sickness.

—ROSALIO MOISES,
YAQUI

On This Date in
Native American History

May 15, 1978: Having their federal tribe recognition stripped from them years before, which officially determined the Modoc, Wyandot, Peoria, and Ottawa Indian tribes of Oklahoma extinct (according to the United States government), their status as a living and breathing tribe was reinstated.

May 16

*It is the general belief of the Indians
that after a man dies his spirit is somewhere on the earth or in the sky. We
do not know exactly where, but we
are sure that his spirit still lives. So it is
with Wakan tanka. We believe that he
is everywhere yet he is to us as the
spirits of our friends whose voices we
can not hear.*

—CHASED-BY-BEARS,
SANTEE-YANKTONAI SIOUX, 1843–1915

May 17

Let the person I serve express his thanks according to his own bringing up and his sense of humor.

—OHIYESA (CHARLES EASTMAN),
SANTEE SIOUX, 1858–1939

Did You Know?

One of the most persistent stereotypes of the Native American Indians relates to tipis. Contrary to popular opinion, the tipi was not home to all Native Americans prior to—and following—the settlement of the white man. In fact, it was primarily used by the Plains people, who needed a sturdy home that could be torn down and packed rather quickly.

May 18

*Great Spirit, Great Spirit, my Grand-
father, all over the earth the faces of
living things are all alike. Look upon
these faces of children without number
and with children in their arms that
they may face the winds and walk the
good road to the day of quiet.*

—BLACK ELK, OGLALA SIOUX, 1863–1950

Did You Know?

Since before 2000 B.C., Native peoples
have used tobacco during ceremonies
and sacred rituals, and as an offering to
the Earth or Earth's Creator or to other
spiritual beings. Traditionally, the herb
may have been smoked in a pipe during
council meeting, or, for tribes such as
the Ojibway, it may have been used
prior to a vision quest. Often, smoking
tobacco prefaced a tribal action. The
people did not move forward, nor
would an important decision be made,
without first using tobacco to clear the
mind and to consult the spirits.

May 19

*If the white man wants to live in peace
with the Indian, he can live in peace . . .
Treat all men alike. Give them all the
same law. Give them all an even chance
to live and grow. All men were made by
the same Great Spirit Chief. They are all
brothers.*

—CHIEF JOSEPH
(HIN-MAH-TOO-YAH-LAT-KEKT), NEZ PERCE,
1840–1904

May 20

While living I want to live well.
I know I have to die sometime, but
even if the heavens were to fall on me
I want to do what is right . . .

—GOYATHLAY (GERONIMO),
APACHE MEDICINE MAN AND WAR CHIEF,
1829–1909

On This Date in
Native American History

May 20, 1972: 21,000 acres from the
Gifford Pinchot National Forest were
returned to the Yakima Indians of
Washington state by President Richard
M. Nixon.

May 21

Much has been said of the want of what you term "civilization" among the Indians. Many proposals have been made to adopt your laws, your religion, your manners, and your customs. We would be better pleased with beholding the good effects of these doctrines in your own practices, than with hearing you talk about them. You say, "Why do not the Indians till the ground and live as we do?" May we not ask with equal propriety, "Why do not the white people hunt and live as we do?"

—OLD TASSEL,
CHEROKEE

May 22

When temptation comes, I don't say, "Yes," and I don't say, "No." I say, "Later." I just keep walking the Red Road—down the middle. When you're in the middle, you don't go to either extreme. You allow both sides to exist.

—Dr. A. C. Ross (Ehanamani), Lakota

Did You Know?

Dreamcatchers are not supposed to be placed around car mirrors. They serve a cultural importance that places them only above one's bed, where one sleeps.

May 23

Good words do not last long unless they amount to something. Words do not pay for my dead people. Words do not pay for my country, now overrun by white men. They do not protect my father's grave. They do not pay for all my horses and cattle. Good words will not give me back my children. Good words will not make good the promise of your War Chief. Good words will not give my people good health and stop them from dying. Good words will not get my people a home where they can live in peace and take care of themselves. I am tired of talk that comes to nothing. It makes my heart sick when I remember all the good words and all the broken promises. There has been too much talking by men who had no right to talk.

—CHIEF JOSEPH
(HIN-MAH-TOO-YAH-LAT-KEKT), NEZ PERCE,
1840–1904

May 24

*Friendship between two persons
depends upon the patience of one.*

—NATIVE AMERICAN PROVERB

A Native to Know

Colorado Senator Ben Nighthorse
Campbell was born in 1933 to a
Northern Cheyenne mother and a
Portuguese father. Raised in California, he is the first Native American
Indian to serve in the U.S. Senate in
more than 60 years. Campbell serves
on the Indian Affairs Committee, and
is also a published author, rancher,
and jewelry designer.

May 25

From Wakan-Tanka, the Great Mystery, comes all power. It is from Wakan-Tanka that the holy man has wisdom and the power to heal and make holy charms. Man knows that all healing plants are given by Wankan-Tanka, therefore they are holy. So too is the buffalo holy, because it is the gift of Wakan-Tanka.

—FLAT IRON,
OGLALA SIOUX, LATE 19TH CENTURY

May 26

*The Black Hills are the house
of gold for our Indians.
We watch it to get rich.*

—LITTLE BEAR

Did You Know?

For many indigenous tribes, it was a common practice to sing a song—called a Death Chant—while dying. Kiowa leader Satank sang his death song in 1871 to show that he knew he was about to cross over.

May 27

My father, you have made promises to me and to my children. If the promises had been made by a person of no standing, I should not be surprised to see the promises fail. But you, who are so great in riches and in power, I am astonished that I do not see your fulfilled promises. I would have been better pleased if you had never made such promises, than that you should have made them and not performed them . . .

—SHINGUACONSE (LITTLE PINE)

May 28

Listen to all the teachers in the woods.
Watch the trees, the animals and all
living things—you'll learn more from
them than from books.

—JOE COYHIS,
STOCKBRIDGE-MUNSEE

Did You Know?

The bald eagle, the national symbol of
the United States, was first the symbol
of the Iroquois Nation.

May 29

That is the way with us Indians,
goods and earth are not equal.
Goods are for using the earth.

—YELLOW SERPENT

Did You Know?

"Alabama" means "I am one who
works the land, harvests food from it"
in Choctaw.

May 30

His brave warriors will be with us,
a bristling wall of strength.

—Chief Seattle (Seathl),
Duwamish-Suquamish, 1785–1866

A Native to Know

Chief Seattle was born near Puget
Sound in 1785. He was well known for
his beliefs in peace, friendship, and
love of the land. A strong advocate of
his people, Chief Seattle is considered
one of the most beloved Native leaders
of all time.

May 31

I believe much trouble would be saved if we opened our hearts more. I will tell you in my way how the Indian sees things. The white man has more words to tell you how they look to him, but it does not require many words to speak the truth.

—CHIEF JOSEPH
(HIN-MAH-TOO-YAH-LAT-KEKT), NEZ PERCE,
1840–1904

Red Road Ethic 6
Respect

Respect is to be given for all beings placed upon this earth by the Creator.

Respect is to be given to elders, who are rich with wisdom.

Respect one's privacy, thoughts, and wishes.

Respect human siblings by only speaking of their good qualities.

Respect one's personal space and belongings.

Respect another's spiritual path and do not judge their choices.

Trouble no one about their religion; respect others in their view, and demand that they respect yours. Love your life, perfect your life, and beautify all things in your life. Seek to make your life long and its purpose in the service of your people. Prepare a noble death song for the day when you go over the great divide. Always give a word or a sign of salute when meeting or passing a friend, even a stranger, when in a lonely place. Show respect to all people and bow to no one . . .

—TECUMSEH, SHAWNEE, 1768–1813

JUNE

JUNE POTAWATOMI MOON:
MONTH OF THE TURTLE

*Summer—known as Cohattayough
in Powhatan—is upon us.*

June 1

I know of no species of plant, bird, or animal that were exterminated until the coming of the white man. The white man considered natural animal life upon this continent, as "pests." There is no word in the Lakota vocabulary with the English meaning of this word . . . [the Indian] was . . . kin to all living things and he gave to all creatures equal rights with himself. [To the white man] the worth and right to live were his. Forests were mowed down, the buffalo were exterminated, the beaver driven to extinction and his wonderfully constructed dams dynamited. Springs, streams, and lakes that lived no longer ago than my boyhood have dried, and a whole people harassed to degradation and death. The white man has become the symbol of extinction for all things natural to this continent. Between him and the animal there is no rapport.

—LUTHER STANDING BEAR,
OGLALA SIOUX, 1868–1937

June 2

Last night I saw the sun set for the last time, and its light shine upon the tree tops, and the land, and the water, that I am never to look upon again.

—MENEWA, CREEK,
PRIOR TO HIS FORCED MARCH WESTWARD IN 1836

On This Date in
Native American History

June 2, 1924: All American Indians were granted U.S. citizenship.

June 3

My father went on talking to me in a low voice. This is how our people always talk to their children, so low and quiet, the child thinks he is dreaming. But he never forgets.

—MARIA CHONA,
PAPAGO

On This Date in
Native American History

June 3, 1948: Korczak Ziolkowski began his prodigious task of sculpting the Crazy Horse Monument from a mountain near Mount Rushmore, South Dakota.

June 4

Wolf I am, Everything . . .
in darkness will be good . . .
In light because Maheo . . .
Whenever I search Protects us
. . .Wherever I run Ea ea ea ho.

—SONG OF A CHEYENNE SCOUT

June 5

*The Great Spirit first made the world,
and next the flying animals, and
found all things good and pros-
perous—He is immortal and ever-
lasting. After finishing the flying
animals, He came down on earth, and
there stood. Then He made different
kinds of trees and weeds of all sorts,
and people of every kind. He made the
spring and other seasons, and the
weather suitable for planting . . . When
the Great Spirit had made the earth
and its animals, He went into the great
lakes, where He breathed as easily as
anywhere else and then made the different kinds of fish . . . He is the cause
of all things that exist, and it is very
wicked to go against His will . . . Some
of us now keep the seventh day; but
I wish to quit it, for the Great Spirit
made it for others, but not for the
Indians, who are out everyday to
attend to their business.*

—CORNPLANTER,
SENECA, 1736–1836

June 6

These were not our ways. We kept the laws we made and lived our religion. We have never been able to understand the white man, who fools nobody but himself.

—CHIEF PLENTY COUPS,
CROW, 1848–1932

On This Date in
Native American History

June 6, 1971: Forty American Indians protested for rights atop Mount Rushmore National Memorial.

June 7

Indian names were either character-istic nicknames given in a playful spirit, deed names, birth names, or such as have a religious and symbolic meaning . . . A man of forcible char-acter, with a fine war record, usually bears the name of the buffalo or bear, lightning or some dread natural force. Another of more peaceful nature may be called Swift Bird or Blue Sky . . .

—OHIYESA (CHARLES EASTMAN),
SANTEE SIOUX, 1858–1939

In Remembrance

Of Chief Seattle, who crossed over on June 7, 1866.

June 8

We are part fire, and part dream.
We are the physical mirroring of
Miaheyyun, the Total Universe, upon
this earth, our Mother. We are here to
experience. We are a movement of
hand within millions of seasons, a
wink of touching within millions and
millions of sun fires. And we speak with
the Mirroring of the Sun. The wind is
the Spirit of these things. The force of
the natural things of this world are
brought together within the whirlwind.

—FIRE DOG,
CHEYENNE

In Remembrance

Of Chief Cochise, who crossed over on
June 8, 1874.

June 9

In the beginning of all things, wisdom and knowledge were with the animals, for Tirawa, the One Above, did not speak directly to man. He sent certain animals to tell men that he showed himself through the beast, and that from them, and from the stars and the sun and moon should man learn . . . all things tell of Tirawa.

—LETAKOTS-LESA (GRAY EAGLE CHIEF),
PAWNEE, 19TH CENTURY

June 10

American Indians share a history rich in diversity, integrity, culture, and tradition. It is also rich in tragedy, deceit, and genocide. As the world learns of these atrocities and cries out for justice for all people everywhere, no human being should ever have to fear for his or her life because of their political or religious beliefs. We are in this together, my friends, the rich, the poor, the red, white, black, brown, and yellow. We share responsibility for Mother Earth and those who live and breathe upon her. Never forget that.

—LEONARD PELTIER,
NATIVE AMERICAN RIGHTS ACTIVIST

June 11

*The Native vision, the gift of seeing
truly, with wonder and delight into the
natural world, is informed by a certain attitude of reverence and respect.
It is a matter of extrasensory as well as
sensory perception. In addition to the
eye, it involves the intelligence, the
instinct, and the imagination. It is the
perception not only of objects and
forms but also of essences and ideals.*

—N. SCOTT MOMADAY,
KIOWA, 1934–

On This Date in
Native American History

June 11, 1971: The 19-month occupation
of Alcatraz Island ended when the last
of the protesting American Indians—six
men, five children, and four women—
were removed by federal marshals.

June 12

*There is a dignity about the
social intercourse of old Indians
which reminds me of a stroll
through a winter forest.*

—COCHISE

*Do you know or can you believe that
sometimes the idea obtrudes . . .
whether it has been well that I have
sought civilization with its bothersome
concomitants and whether it would
not be better even now to return to
the darkness and most sacred wilds
(if any such can be found) of our
country and there to vegetate and
expire silently, happily and forgotten ·
as do the birds of the air and the
beasts of the field. The thought is a
happy one but perhaps impracticable.*

—ELY S. PARKER,
SENECA-IROQUOIS, 1828–1895

June 13

So I know that it is a good thing I am going to do; and because no good thing can be done by any man alone, I will first make an offering and send a voice to the spirit world, that it may help me to be true. See I fill this sacred pipe with the bark of the red willow; but before we smoke it you must see how it is made and what it means. These four ribbons hanging here on the stem are the four quarters of the universe. The black one is for the west where the thunder beings live to send us rain; the white one for the north, whence comes the great white cleansing wind; the red one for the east, whence springs the light and where the morning star lives to give men wisdom; the yellow for the south, whence comes the summer and the power to grow.

—BLACK ELK,
OGLALA SIOUX, 1863–1950

June 14

Do not grieve. Misfortunes will happen to the wisest and best of men. Death will come and always out of season. It is the command of the Great Spirit, and all nations and people must obey. What is past and cannot be prevented should not be grieved for . . . Misfortunes do not flourish particularly in our path. They grow everywhere.

—OMAHA CHIEF BIG ELK,
IN A FUNERAL SPEECH FOR
BLACK BUFFALO, HEROIC INDIAN LEADER,
DELIVERED JUNE 14, 1815,
AT A GREAT COUNCIL AT PORTAGE DES SIOUX.

Red Road Lesson 6
Four Sacred Medicines

Though all plants are purposeful and important, four plants are sacred:

1. Tobacco is used in the offering of prayer to the Great Spirit. The smoke contains the prayers that are then lifted skyward.

2. Cedar purifies; good fortune will come your way if you carry cedar in your shoes.

3. Sage cleans the body and repels negative energy.

4. Sweetgrass also purifies and is carried for positive.

So I know that it is a good thing I am going to do; and because no good thing can be done by any man alone, I will first make an offering and send a voice to the spirit world that it may help me to be true. See, I fill this sacred pipe with the bark of the red willow; but before we smoke it you must see what it means. These four ribbons hanging here on the stem are the four quarters of the universe.

—BLACK ELK, OGLALA SIOUX, 1863–1950

June 15

My friends, how desperately do we need to be loved and to love. Love is something you and I must have. We must have it because our spirit feeds upon it. We must have it because without it we become weak and faint. Without love our self-esteem weakens. Without it our courage fails. Without love we can no longer look out confidently at the world. We turn inward and begin to feed upon our own personalities, and little by little we destroy ourselves. With it we are creative. With it we march tirelessly. With it, and with it alone, we are able to sacrifice for others.

—Chief Dan George,
Coast Salish, 1899–1981

June 16

During the first year a newly married couple discovers whether they can agree with each other and can be happy—if not, they part, and look for other partners. If we were to live together and disagree, we should be as foolish as the whites. No indiscretion can banish a woman from her parental lodge. It makes no difference how many children she may bring home; she is always welcome. The kettle is over the fire to feed them.

—BLACK ELK,
OGLALA SIOUX, 1863–1950

June 17

The Indians were religious from the first moments of life. From the moment of the mother's recognition that she had conceived the mother's spiritual influence was supremely important. . . . Silence and isolation are the rule of life for the expectant mother. She wanders prayerful in the stillness of great woods, and to her poetic mind the imminent birth of her child prefigures the advent of a hero. And when the day of days in her life dawns—the day in which there is to be a new life, the miracle of whose making has been entrusted to her—she seeks no human aid. She has been trained and prepared in body and mind for this. Childbirth is best met alone, where no curious embarrass her, where all nature says to her spirit: "It's love! It's love! The fulfilling of life!" She feels the endearing warmth of it and hears its soft breathing. It is still a part of herself, and no look of a lover could be sweeter than its deep, trusting gaze.

—Ohiyesa (Charles Eastman),
Santee Sioux, 1858–1939

June 18

My breath—this is what I call my song, for it is just as necessary to me to sing as it is to me to breathe. I will sing this song, a song that is strong . . . Songs are thoughts, sung out with the breath when people are moved by great forces and ordinary speech no longer suffices. Man is moved just like the ice floe sailing here and there out in the current. His thoughts are driven by a flowing force when he feels joy, when he feels sorrow. Thoughts can wash over him like a flood, making his blood come in gasps, then it will happen that we, who always think we are small, will feel still smaller. And we will fear to use words. But it will happen that the words we need will come of themselves. When the words we want to use shoot up of themselves—we get a new song.

—Orpingalik, Netsilingmuit

June 19

We do not worship the Great Spirit as the white people do, but we believe that the forms of worship are indifferent to the Great Spirit.

—RED JACKET (SAGOYEWATHA),
SENECA, 1811

Did You Know?

Indigenous cultures often had birth rituals that involved where the child was born, how the child was born, what was done with the umbilical cord, and the rules that were set for the first few weeks of the child's life. These rules and rituals were to ensure the safety of the mother, and also the safety, success, and luck of the child and of the entire family.

June 20

Oh, the comfort, the inexpressible comfort of feeling safe with a person, having neither to weigh thoughts . . . but pouring them all out, just as they are, chaff and grain together, certain that a faithful hand will take and sift them, keep what is worth keeping, and with a breath of kindness, blow the rest away.

—ANONYMOUS SHOSHONE TRIBAL MEMBER

June 21

*The Great Spirit told me to tell the
Indians that he had made them,
and made the world that he placed
them on to do good, not evil.*

—TENSKWATAWA (THE PROPHET),
SHAWNEE, 1808

On This Date in
Native American History

June 21, 1968: Nearly 100 American
Indians demonstrated outside the Bureau of Indian Affairs to show their support for the Poor People's Campaign in
Washington, D.C., which was conceived and organized by Martin Luther
King Jr.

June 22

*The land known as the Black Hills
is considered by the Indians as
the center of their land.*

—RUNNING ANTELOPE,
FOLLOWING LT. COL. GEORGE A. CUSTER'S
1874 BLACK HILLS GOLD EXPEDITION

Did You Know?

The 1828 *Cherokee Phoenix,* the first
American Indian newspaper, was published in both Cherokee and English.

June 23

A warrior who had more than needed would make a feast. He went around and invited the old and needy. The man who could thank the food, some worthy old medicine man or warrior said, "Look to the old, they are worthy of old age. They have seen their days and proven themselves. With the help of the Great Spirit they have attained a ripe old age. At this age the old can predict or give knowledge or wisdom whatever it is: it is so. At the end is a cane. You and your family shall get to where the cane is.

—BLACK ELK,
OGLALA SIOUX, 1863–1950

June 24

Your religious calling was written on plates of stone by the flaming finger of an angry God. Our religion was established by the traditions of our ancestors, the dreams of our elders that are given to them in the silent hours of night by the Great Spirit.

—CHIEF WHITE CLOUD,
IOWA

A Native to Know

Carol Geddes, Inland Tlingit, was born in a small Yukon village in 1945. She is best known for the more than 20 movies she has produced, including the highly acclaimed *Doctor, Lawyer, Indian Chief* (1986) which won an award at the 1988 National Educational Film and Video Festival.

June 25

When I was a young man I went to a medicine-man for advice concerning my future. The medicine-man said: "I have not much to tell you except to help you understand this earth on which you live . . . If a man is to succeed on the hunt or the warpath he must not be governed by his inclination but by an understanding of the ways of animals and of his natural surroundings, gained through close observation. The earth is large, and on it live many animals. The earth is under the protection of something which at times becomes visible to the eye."

—Lone Man (Isna-la-wica), Teton Sioux, late 19th century

June 26

I believe that ancient tribal cultures have important lessons to teach the rest of the world about the interconnectedness of all living things and the simple fact that our very existence is dependent upon the natural world we are rapidly destroying.

—Wilma Mankiller,
first woman elected
Cherokee deputy chief, 1991

June 27

*He who is present at a wrongdoing
and lifts not a hand to prevent it,
is as guilty as the wrongdoers.*

—ESTAMAZA, OMAHA, 1818–1888

Did You Know?

The Arawak people of the Lesser
Antilles developed a language just for
females after many women were cap-
tured and enslaved, and the men killed.

June 28

We believed in a power that was higher than all people and all the created world, and we called this power the Man-Above. We believed in some power in the world that governed everything that grew, and we called this power Mother-Earth. We believed in the power of the Sun, of the Night-Sun or Moon, of the Morning Star, and of the Four Old Men who direct the winds and the rains and the seasons and give us the breath of life. We believed that everything created is holy and has some party of the power that is over all.

—CARL SWEEZY,
ARAPAHO, 1881–1953

June 29

*Though we are powerful and
strong, and we know how to fight,
we do not wish to fight.*

—CHEROKEE ADAGE

Did You Know?

"Arkansas" means "land of the south
wind people" in Sioux.

June 30

I appeal to any white man to say if he ever entered Logan's cabin hungry, and he gave him not meat; if he ever came cold and naked, and he clothed him not. During the course of the last long and bloody war, Logan remained idle in his cabin, an advocate for peace.

—CHIEF LOGAN (TAHGAHJUTE), CAYUGA, ABOUT 1774

THE SOUTHERN
JOURNEY OF SUMMER

Green is a common color for summer. It represents the lush grass and the emerald fullness of nature's forest. Summer is warm, comforting, and a time to relax and enjoy the sunshine. It's a perfect opportunity to build community ties and participate in summer solstice events such as bonfires and cookouts. South is representative of living willfully, passionately, and with love.

Direction: South
Season: Summer
Color: Green

Great Spirit, Great Spirit, my Grandfather, all over the earth the faces of living things are all alike . . . Look upon these faces of children without number and with children in their arms, that they may face the winds and walk the good road to the day of the quiet.

—BLACK ELK,
OGLALA SIOUX, 1863–1950

JULY

JULY ZUNI MOON:
MOON WHEN LIMBS OF TREES
ARE BROKEN BY FRUIT

Red Road Ethic 7
Speak the Truth

Speak only the truth and do right always. You are what you say . . . and what you say needs to be honest, forthright, and of your own personal belief. Without truth you cannot achieve inner balance—balance within yourself, with other beings, with Mother Earth, and with the Creator.

Good words do not last long until they amount to something.

—CHIEF JOSEPH
(HIN-MAH-TOO-YAH-LAT-KEKT), NEZ PERCE,
1840–1904

July 1

The man who sat on the ground in his tipi meditating on life and its meaning, accepting the kinship of all creatures and acknowledging unity with the universe of things, was infusing into his being the true essence of civilization.

—LUTHER STANDING BEAR,
OGLALA SIOUX, 1868–1937

July 2

I was going around the world with the clouds when God spoke to my thought and told me to . . . be at peace with all.

—COCHISE,
CHIRICAHUA APACHE TRIBAL LEADER,
1812–1874

Did You Know?

"Illinois" means "men" or "warriors" in Algonquin.

July 3

*Indians . . . know better how to
live . . . Nobody can be in good health
if he does not have all the time fresh
air, sunshine and good water.*

—Chief Flying Hawk,
Oglala Sioux, 1852–1931

Did You Know?

The majority of Native Americans are of mixed heritage. A "full-blooded" Indian is very rare. Native people may have European, Asian, or African blood in their lineage. Others mix with other Native nationalities, some of which are not federally recognized.

July 4

*The traditions of our people are
handed down from father to son.
The Chief is considered to be the most
learned, and the leader of the tribe.
The Doctor, however, is thought to have
more inspiration. He is supposed to be
in communion with spirits . . . He
cures the sick by the laying of hands,
and prayers and incantations and
heavenly songs. He infuses new life
into the patient, and performs most
wonderful feats of skill in his practice
. . . He clothes himself in the skins of
young innocent animals, such as the
fawn, and decorates himself with the
plumage of harmless birds, such as the
dove and hummingbird . . .*

—SARAH WINNEMUCCA,
PAIUTE, 1844–1891

July 5

*Flowers are for our souls to enjoy;
not for our bodies to wear. Leave
them alone and they will live out
their lives and reproduce themselves
as the Great Gardener intended.*

—SIOUX ADAGE

Did You Know?

Tribal women play an important and
respected role in their communities.
Women and men had specific duties,
and their roles in the tribe are valued.
Women's duties are not degrading, nor
are they considered an easier task.

July 6

You sent for us; we came . . .

—TALL BULL (HOTOAKHIHOOIS),
CHEYENNE LEADER

Did You Know?
Indian Pledge of Allegiance

I pledge allegiance to my Tribe,
to the democratic principles of the
Republic
and to the individual freedoms
borrowed from the Iroquois and
Choctaw Confederacies,
as incorporated in the United States
Constitution,
so that my forefathers
shall not have died in vain.

This pledge was first presented in 1993 during the opening address of the National Congress of American Indian Tribal-States Relations Panel in Nevada.

July 7

*. . . if we cut ourselves, the blood will
be red—and so with the whites it is the
same, though their skin be white . . .
I am of another nation, when I speak
you do not understand me. When you
speak, I do not understand you.*

—Spokan Gary,
Middle Spokan chief, 1811–1892

Did You Know?

Ancient Native people had no written
language but did keep tribal records via
symbols inscribed on stone, bark, hide,
and pottery. Many of these inscriptions
still survive today.

July 8

We have reason to glory in the achievements of our ancestors.

—O NO'SA

On This Date in Native American History

July 8, 1970: President Richard M. Nixon promised new services to Native people and a strengthening of their community. He then returned the sacred land of Blue Lake to the Taos Pueblo Indians.

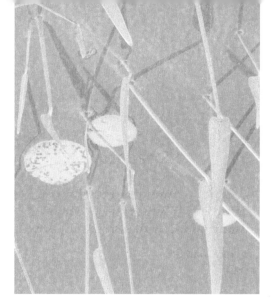

July 9

*One does not sell the
land people walk on.*

—CRAZY HORSE,
SEPTEMBER 23, 1875

Did You Know?

Warbonnets were worn by many of the
Plains tribes prior to setting off for battle.

July 10

When a man does a piece of work which is admired by all we say that it is wonderful; but when we see the changes of day and night, the sun, the moon, and the stars in the sky, and the changing seasons upon the earth, with their ripening fruits, anyone must realize that it is the work of someone more powerful than man.

—Chased-by-Bears,
Santee-Yanktonai Sioux, 1843–1915

July 11

"Ea Nigada Qusdi Idadadvhn"
(all my relations in creation)

—CHEROKEE ADAGE

On This Date in
Native American History

July 11, 1968: The American Indian Movement (AIM) was founded in Minneapolis, Minnesota.

July 12

Once I was in Victoria, and I saw a very large house. They told me it was a bank and that the white men place their money there to be taken care of, and that by and by they got it back with interest. We are Indians and we have no such bank; but when we have plenty of money or blankets, we give them away to other chiefs and people, and by and by they return them with interest, and our hearts feel good. Our way of giving is our bank.

—Chief Maquinna,
Nootka

July 13

You ask me to plow the ground. Shall I take a knife and tear my mother's bosom? Then when I die she will not take me to her bosom to rest. You ask me to dig for stones! Shall I dig under her skin for bones? Then when I die I cannot enter her body to be born again. You ask me to cut grass and make hay and sell it and be rich like white men, but how dare I cut my mother's hair? I want my people to stay with me here. All the dead men will come to life again. Their spirits will come to their bodies again. We must wait here in the homes of our fathers and be ready to meet them in the bosom of our mother.

—WOVOKA (JACK WILSON),
PAIUTE SPIRITUAL LEADER, c. 1856–1932

July 14

Do not wrong or hate your neighbor;
for it is not he that you wrong;
you wrong yourself.

—Shawnee saying

Did You Know?

Native people of yesterday lived off the entire buffalo. They ate the meat, tongue, liver, and ribs, and boiled the hooves as glue. Sinew was dried and split for bow strings, the bladder was used as a water jug, the skull was adornment, and the hide was used for clothing, blankets, shields, and shelter.

Red Road Lesson 7
The Circle

The Circle is an ancient symbol that represents eternity and life of all beings upon Mother Earth. The almighty sun is round, Mother Earth is round, and the cycle of life—from birth to death/rebirth—is also round. It represents unification and fulfillment, and is a powerful visual tool of the Medicine Wheel.

You have noticed that everything an Indian does is in a circle, and that is because the Power of the World always works in circles, and everything tries to be round . . . The Sky is round, and I have heard that the earth is round like a ball, and so are all the stars. The wind, in its greatest power, whirls. Birds make their nest in circles, for theirs is the same religion as ours . . . Even the seasons form a great circle in their changing, and always come back again to where they were. The life of a man is a circle from childhood to childhood, and so it is in everything where power moves.

—BLACK ELK, OGLALA SIOUX, 1863–1950

July 15

Brother, you say there is but one way to worship and serve the Great Spirit. If there is but one religion, why do you white people differ so much about it? Why not all agreed, as you can all read the Book?

—RED JACKET (SAGOYEWATHA),
SENECA, C. 1752–1830

A Native to Know

Seneca Chief Red Jacket was born in present-day New York near Seneca Lake in 1752. When asked about his being a warrior, he replied, "A warrior? I am an orator. I was born an orator!" Red Jacket, called this because he usually wore a red military jacket given to him by a British army acquaintance, was gifted in speech and in his ability to deal peacefully with non-Natives. Many of his speeches have been recorded and remembered.

July 16

In all your official acts, self-interest shall be cast aside. You shall look and listen to the welfare of the whole people and have always in view, not only the present but the coming generations— the unborn of the future Nation.

—DEKANAWIDAH, IROQUOIS, C. 1300

Did You Know?

You must never refer to Native dress as a "costume," especially at special exhibits and powwows. This term is considered offensive. The proper term is "outfit" or "dress."

July 17

There were many whites, who, after having tried it, expressed a preference for the free but hazardous life of savagery to the more restrained life of civilization . . .

—ALEXANDER HENRY,
A YOUNG AMERICAN TRADER, WHO LIVED
AMONG THE INDIANS IN 1763 AND 1764

Did You Know?

"Michigan" comes from the Chippewa word meaning "great water."

July 18

The wind that gave our grandfather his first breath also receives his last sigh. And the wind must also give our children the spirit of life.

—CHIEF SEATTLE (SEATHL),
DUWAMISH-SUQUAMISH, 1785–1866

Did You Know?

In the 19th century, many tipis were painted, and their designs would be handed down from generation to generation.

July 19

In the last place . . . we are bound . . . to watch for each other's preservation.

—CANASSATEGO,
ONONDAGA, 1742

On This Date in
Native American History

July 19, 1881: When he surrendered in Dakota Territory, Sitting Bull said, "Let it be recorded that I am the last man of my people to lay down my gun."

July 20

When a man does a piece of work which is admired by all we say that it is wonderful; but when we see the changes of day and night, the sun, the moon, and the stars in the sky, and the changing seasons upon the earth, with their ripening fruits, anyone must realize that it is the work of someone more powerful than man.

—CHASED-BY-BEARS,
SANTEE-YANKTONAI SIOUX,
1843–1915

July 21

Walk on a rainbow trail,
walk on a trail of song,
and all about you will be beauty.
There is a way out of every dark mist,
over a rainbow trail.

—Navajo song

July 22

*There are many secrets which
the Great Mystery will disclose only
to the most worthy. Only those who
seek him [in] fasting and in solitude
will receive his signs.*

—UNCHEEDAH,
SANTEE SIOUX

A Native to Know

Pauline Johnson was a Mohawk poet
born to an English mother and a
Mohawk chief father in 1861 at the Six
Nations Reserve in Ontario. Her first
book of poetry was published in 1895;
she later successfully toured the Americas giving readings, and published five
additional works.

July 23

We acknowledge first the
goodness of Wankan Tanka . . .
we are sure his spirit lives.

—CHASED-BY-BEARS,
SANTEE-YANKTONAI SIOUX, 1843–1915

On This Date in
Native American History

July 23, 1999: Nearly 900 bands of
Native nations met at the Assembly
of First Nations and the National
Congress of American Indians to
build an alliance between indigenous people in Canada, the United
States, Mexico, and South America.

July 24

*They speak of the mysteries of
the light of day by which the
earth and all living things that
dwell thereon are influenced.*

—Playful Calf

On This Date in
Native American History

July 24, 1977: A 200-year-old debate
between Comanche and Ute nations
regarding hunting rights was officially settled. More than 2,000 members participated in a traditional
ceremony that included smoking a
peace pipe.

July 25

There are no such things as emptiness in the world. Even in the sky there were no vacant places. Everywhere there was life, visible and invisible, and every object possessed something that would be good for us to have also—even to the stones . . . The world teemed with life and wisdom; there was no complete solitude for the Lakota.

—LUTHER STANDING BEAR,
OGLALA SIOUX, 1868–1937

July 26

We believed in one God, the Great Spirit. We believed in our own kind of Ten Commandments. And we behaved as though we believed in them.

—Vine Deloria Sr., Yankton Sioux, 1901–1990

A Native missionary priest on South Dakota Indian reservations, Vine Deloria Sr. was instrumental in his advocacy work for Native people. Vine Deloria Jr. wrote *Custer Died for Your Sins* and *God Is Red*.

July 27

Almost every evening a myth, or a true story of some deed done in the past, was narrated by one of the parents or grandparents, while the boy listened with parted lips and glistening eyes . . .

—OHIYESA (CHARLES EASTMAN),
SANTEE SIOUX, 1858–1939

Did You Know?

To the Haudenosaunee, the eagle is the protector of peace, sitting upon the Tree of Peace to sound alarm when danger is near.

July 28

Oh, Eagle, come with wings
outspread in sunny skies.
Oh, Eagle, come and bring us peace,
thy gentle peace.
Oh, Eagle, come and give new life
to us who pray.
Remember the circle of the sky, the
stars, and the brown eagle,
the great life of the Sun,
the young within the nest.
Remember the sacredness of things.

—Pawnee prayer

Did You Know?

Often, in speech, prayer, or song, Native Americans may give praise to the Great Spirit and to all Native relations including the two-legged, four-legged, and winged ones. This is common practice, since most Native beliefs center around the fact that all living beings are brothers and sisters, and all are equal in the eyes of the Creator.

July 29

*Our fathers gave us many laws,
which they had learned from their
fathers. Those laws were good. They
told us to treat all men as they
treated us, that we should never be
the first to break a bargain, that it
was a disgrace to tell a lie, that we
should only speak the truth . . .*

—Chief Joseph
(Hin-mah-too-yah-lat-kekt), Nez
Perce, 1840–1904

July 30

We do not know what may happen today, but let us act as though we were the Seven Stars (Big Dipper) in the sky that live forever. Go with me as far as you can, and I will go with you while there is breath in my body.

—CHIEF PLENTY COUPS,
CROW, 1848–1932

Did You Know?

The word "squaw" is considered extremely derogatory to Native women and should *never* be used in their presence or in reference to them.

July 31

*Just what Power is I cannot explain,
for it is beyond my comprehension.
Those who seek it go alone that they
may be tested for worthiness. It is a gift
to be bestowed not only for virtue but
for prayer and courage.*

—VICTORIO,
MIMBRES APACHE, 1820–1880

A Native to Know

Victorio was chief of the Ojo Caliente
Apache and at one time served under
Apache Mangas Coloradas. Victorio
was an adamant fighter for his people
and used physical force when necessary. It took an army of more than
2,000 soldiers to defeat the brilliant
strategist and his people, numbering
fewer than 200.

August

August Hopi Moon:
Paamuya: Joyful Moon

Red Road Ethic 8
Reject Materialism

When one is materialistic, one is not right with the Red Road. To value and appreciate what you have and to know that you are loved and safe under the limbs of the Tree of Life is to reject materialism and to live a life of virtue and appreciation. Materialism only fills your heart with envy and greed, while appreciation breeds contentment, balance, and true happiness.

. . . These are my young men. I am their Chief. Look among them and see if you can find among them who are rich. They are all poor because they are all honest.

—RED DOG,
OGLALA SIOUX, 1870

August 1

What is man without the beasts? If all the beasts were gone, men would die from great loneliness of spirit, for whatever happens to the beasts also happens to man. All things are connected. Whatever befalls the earth befalls the children of the earth.

—CHIEF SEATTLE (SEATHL),
DUWAMISH-SUQUAMISH, 1785–1866

Did You Know?

"Oklahoma" is a Choctaw word meaning "Red Men."

August 2

*Each one must learn for himself
the highest wisdom. It cannot
be taught in words.*

—SMOWHALA, WANAPUM

Did You Know?

Most Native nations have two or more names for their tribe. One was given to them by Europeans, while the second is the people's original tribal name, which had a specific meaning. Here are a few tribal names and their meanings:

Apache:	Enemy
Cayuga:	People at the mucky land
Cherokee:	People of different speech
Fox:	Red Earth People
Hopi:	Peaceful Ones
Lakota:	Friend
Omaha:	Upstream people or people going against the current
Powhatan:	Falls in a current of water
Yuki:	Stranger

August 3

The Crow country is good country.
The Great Spirit has put it exactly
in the right place; while you are in
it you fare well; whenever you go
out of it, which ever way you travel,
you fare worse . . . There is no
country like Crow country.

—ARAPOOSH,
CROW, 1833

On This Date in
Native American History

August 3, 1990: November was officially declared "National American
Indian Heritage Month" by Congress.

August 4

The Cherokee lives as a natural part of his environment and strives to complement it, not subdue or dominate it. It's an Indian philosophy that is playing an increasing role in everyone's life now that we realize that natural resources are limited and imbalance between man's technology and nature is perilously close to disaster.

—HUEY P. LONG,
CHEROKEE

August 5

Men die but live again in the real world of Wakan-Tanka, where there is nothing but the spirits of all things; and this true life we may know here on earth if we purify our bodies and minds thus coming closer to Wakan-Tanka who is all-purity.

—BLACK ELK,
OGLALA SIOUX, 1863–1950

In Remembrance

Of Lower Brulé Sioux leader Spotted Tail, who crossed over on August 5, 1881, at the age of 68.

August 6

There is a special magic and holiness about the girl and woman. There are the bringers of life to the people, and the teachers of the little children.

—SWEET MEDICINE,
CHEYENNE

On This Date in
Native American History

August 6, 1975: President Gerald Ford signed into law an act granting non-English-speaking citizens, including American Indians, the right to vote in more than one language.

August 7

We must truly honor what is past,
when we seek in our changed
conditions to attain the same
proficiency that our fathers showed in
their day and in their lives.

—"Old Keyam" (Edward Ahenakew),
Plains Cree

On This Date in
Native American History

August 7, 1969: Louis Bruce, a Mohawk-
Oglala-Sioux Indian from New York,
was appointed to the position of Commissioner of Indian Affairs by President
Richard M. Nixon and Walter Hickel,
Secretary of the Interior. Bruce was the
third American Indian to be appointed
to this position; the other two were
Robert Bennett and Ely Parker.

August 8

The more you know the more you will trust and the less you will fear.

—Ojibway adage

Did You Know?

A powwow was originally an event held during springtime to celebrate the upcoming season of life, birth, fruition, and renewal. Communities would gather together to sing, conduct religious ceremonies, dance, and connect with friends and family. Today, powwows are an important part of tribal unity, perseverance, and renewal, and are held at all times of the year. Some powwows including singing and competitive dancing, and have food and artwork for sale.

August 9

The lands of the planet call to human-kind for redemption. But it is a redemption of sanity, not a supernatural reclamation project at the end of history. The planet itself calls to the other living species for relief. Religion cannot be kept within the bounds of sermons and scriptures. It is a force in and of itself and it calls for the integration of lands and peoples in harmonious unity. The land waits for those who can discern their rhythms. The peculiar genius of each continent—each river valley, the rugged mountains, the placid lakes—all call for relief from the constant burden of exploitation.

—VINE DELORIA JR., LAKOTA,
1973, FROM HIS BOOK *GOD IS RED*

August 10

Look twice at a two-faced man.

—CHIEF JOSEPH (HIN-MAH-TOO-YAH-LAT-KEKT),
NEZ PERCE, 1840–1904

Did You Know?

The medicine pole used by the Mandans (Plains) was similar to the totem pole used by the northwestern tribes. The medicine pole included various animal symbols, which brought power or good energy to the family and/or community.

August 11

*If you do bad things your children
will follow you and do the same.
If you want to raise good children,
be decent yourself.*

—CHRIS,
MESCALERO APACHE

On This Date in
Native American History

August 11, 1978: Congress enacted the
American Indian Religious Freedom
Act, which lifted the ban from many
Native American religious ceremonies,
including the legendary Ghost Dance.

August 12

Every struggle, whether won or lost, strengthens us for the next to come. It is not good for people to have an easy life. They become weak and inefficient when they cease to struggle. Some need a series of defeats before developing the strength and courage to win a victory.

—Victorio,
Mimbres Apache, 1820–1880

August 13

I shall not speak with fear and trembling. I have never injured you, and innocence can feel no fear.

—BLACK THUNDER, FOX

Did You Know?

Music and singing were a vital element in Native American culture. People chanted and played instruments made from animal hides and bone.

August 14

*When the hearts of the givers are filled
with hate, their gifts are small.*

—CHIEF PLENTY COUPS,
CROW, 1848–1932

On This Date in
Native American History

August 14, 1982: Navajo servicemen
who relayed messages that could not be
deciphered by the Japanese during
World War II were honored by President
Ronald Reagan, who declared today
National Navajo Code Talkers Day.

Red Road Lesson 8
How to Say "I Love You"

Here is how you can say "I love you" in eight different Native American languages.

Cheyenne	*Nemehotâtse*
Chickasaw	*Chiholloli*
Hawaiian	*Aloha I'a Au Oe*
Hopi	*Nu' umi unangwa'ta*
Mohawk	*Konoronhkwa*
Navaho	*Ayor anosh'ni*
Ojibway	*Gi zah gin*
Zuni	*Tom ho' ichema*

Love is something you and I must have. We must have it because our spirit feeds upon it.

—CHIEF DAN GEORGE,
COAST SALISH, 1899–1981

August 15

My people were wise. They never neglected the young or failed to keep before them deeds done by illustrious men of the tribe. Our teachers were willing and thorough. They were our grandfathers, fathers, or uncles. All were quick to praise excellence without speaking a word that might break the spirit of a boy who might be less capable than others. The boy who failed at any lesson got only more lessons, more care, until he was as far as he could go.

—CHIEF PLENTY COUPS,
CROW, 1848–1932

August 16

The smarter a man is the more he needs God to protect him from thinking he knows everything.

—GEORGE WEBB, PIMA,
AUTHOR OF THE 1959 BOOK
A PIMA REMEMBERS

Did You Know?

In 1881, President Chester Arthur authorized official rules forbidding "rites, customs . . . contrary to civilization." And all Native dances, traditional rituals, and spiritual rites also were forbidden.

August 17

Experience is the wisest teacher . . .

—PLEASANT PORTER,
CREEK, 1840–1907

Did You Know?

"Metis" is a term used to classify a group of people of mixed blood, primarily Indian and French.

August 18

*Free yourself from negative influence.
Negative thoughts are the old habits
that gnaw at the roots of the soul.*

—MOSES SHONGO,
SENECA

A Native to Know

Mabel McKay, Long Valley Cache
Creek Pomo basketmaker, prophet,
and physician, was born in California
in 1907. She became one of the best
known traditional basketmakers of her
time, and was the last weaver to create
such traditional work. Prior to her
death in 1993, she taught basketmaking at universities and to her own
people. Her work is showcased in
numerous collections throughout the
United States and in Europe.

August 19

My father, you see us as we are. We are poor. We have but few blankets and little clothing. The great father who made us and gave us this land to live upon, made the buffalo and other game to afford us sustenance; their meat is our only food; with their skins we clothe ourselves and build our lodges. They are our only means of life—food, fuel, and clothing . . . We hear a great trail is to be made through our country. We do not know what this is for; we do not understand it, but we think it will scare away the buffalo.

—OLD BRAVE, ASSINIBOIN,
SPEAKING TO GOVERNOR ISSAC STEVENS, 1853

August 20

It is in peace only that our women and children can enjoy happiness, and increase in numbers.

—CHIEF JOHN ROSS,
CHEROKEE, 1790–1866

On This Date in
Native American History

August 20, 1994: Miracle, the first white female buffalo calf in over a century, was born in Janesville, Wisconsin, to non-Native ranchers. The birth of a white buffalo calf was prophesied by Native people generations ago, and she is seen as a sign of tribal unity and peace by believers all across the country. Thousands pilgrimage to see her, and Miracle received worldwide media attention.

August 21

*One has to face fear or
forever run from it.*

—HAWK,
CROW

On This Date in
Native American History

August 21, 1861: Cherokee Principal
Chief John Ross spoke to his people
about remaining neutral with both
sides in the American Civil War: "While
ready and willing to defend our fire-
sides, let us not make war wantonly
against the authority of the United or
Confederate States, but avoid a conflict
with either, and remain strictly on our
own soil."

August 22

*If you have one hundred people
who live together, and if each one
cares for the rest, there is one mind.*

—SHINING ARROWS,
CROW

On This Date in
Native American History

August 22, 1810: Tecumseh embarked
on a journey to protect his people, fight
for their property rights, and build a
confederacy among his fellow Indians.

August 23

The white man thinks with his head—the Indian thinks with his heart.

—JIMALEE BURTON
(HO-CHEE-NEE), CHEROKEE

On This Date in Native American History

August 23, 1886: Geronimo, the great Chihuahua Apache leader, surrendered to General Nelson A. Miles and agreed to give up arms and live on a reservation, in peace, for the remainder of his days.

August 24

I do not want to settle down in the houses you would build for us. I love to roam over the wild prairies. There I am free and happy. When we sit down, we grow pale and die.

—Satanta (White Bear),
Kiowa, 1830–1878

Did You Know?

Native American spirituality is primarily rooted in the personal experience with nature. Each person is to nurture his or her own path, to form his or her own connections and attachments.

August 25

It is a truth, a melancholy truth,
that the good things which men do
are often buried in the ground,
while their evil deeds are stripped
naked and exposed to the world.

—BLACK THUNDER,
FOX

Did You Know?

Just like other cultures, Native Americans had their own explanations of how and why they—and the Earth—were created, and by whom. Many claim their tribal birth from the womb of Mother Earth, while others give credit to animals or mythological beings.

August 26

In you, as in all men, are natural powers. You have a will. Learn to use it. Make it work for you. Sharpen your senses as you sharpen your knife . . . We can give you nothing. You already possess everything necessary to become great.

—Legendary Dwarf Chief,
Crow

Did You Know?

There were 13 basic housing structures used by Native people: Chickee, Igloo, Pit House, Tipi, Wickiup, Pueblo, Hogan, Wattle and Daub, Longhouse, Wigwam, Plank House, Lean-to, and Earthlodge.

August 27

. . . An Indian who is as bad as a white man could not live in our nation; he would be put to death and eaten by the wolves. The white men are bad schoolmasters; they carry false looks and deal in false actions; they smile in the face of the poor Indian to cheat him; they shake him by the hand to gain his confidence, to make him drunk, to deceive him, to ruin his wife . . . Black Hawk is a true Indian, and disdains to cry like a woman. He feels for his wife, his children and his friends. But he does not care for himself. He cares for his nation, and the Indians. They will suffer. He laments their fate . . . Farewell, my nation! . . . He can do no more. He is near his end. His sun is setting, and will rise no more. Farewell to Black Hawk!

—BLACK HAWK,
FROM HIS SPEECH TO J. M. STREET,
AUGUST 27, 1832

August 28

The color of the skin makes no difference; what is good and just for one is good and just for the other.

—WHITE SHIELD, ARIKARA

Did You Know?

If an eagle feather falls from a dancer's outfit during a dance or powwow, the event stops and a ceremony is quickly performed to restore the feather's power.

August 29

In every human heart there is a deep spiritual hunger for an abiding belief in some future existence. Such a faith stabilizes character, and many of our young people have no such anchor for their souls.

—THOMAS WILDCAT ALFORD, SHAWNEE, 1930

On This Date in Native American History

August 29, 1911: Ishi, the last Yana Indian, was found hiding in Oroville, California.

August 30

Wowienke he iyotam wowa sake (Truth is power).

—LAKOTA ADAGE

Did You Know?

There is an old belief among Native people that 90 percent of all illnesses come from bad feelings, guilt, or negative energy.

August 31

. . . The Earth is our Mother. From her we get our life . . . and our ability to live. It is our responsibility to care for our Mother, and in caring for our Mother, we care for ourselves. Women, all females are the manifestation of Mother Earth in human form. We are her daughters and in my cultural instructions—Minobimaatisiiwin—we are to care for her. I am taught to live in respect for Mother Earth. In Indigenous societies, we are told that Natural Law is the highest law, higher than the law made by nations, states, municipalities and the world bank. That one would do well to live in accordance with Natural Law, with those of our Mother. And in respect for our Mother Earth of our relations— indinawaymuguni took.

—WINONA LaDUKE, OF THE MISSISSIPPI BAND OF THE ANISHINAABE OF THE WHITE EARTH RESERVATION, MINNESOTA, AND A CANDIDATE FOR VICE PRESIDENT IN 2000 UNDER THE GREEN PARTY TICKET, SPEAKING TO AN ASSEMBLY AT THE INDIGENOUS WOMEN'S NETWORK IN BEIJING, CHINA

SEPTEMBER

SEPTEMBER TEWA PUEBLO MOON:
MOON WHEN THE CORN IS TAKEN IN

*Autumn—also known as Pahcotai
in Shawnee—is upon us.*

Red Road Ethic 9
Seek Wisdom

Those who are wise have lived a lifetime with ears open and a willingness to not only experience truth, but to pursue it as well.

Wisdom is gained by:

Listening to your elders. They have walked a longer path than you.

Seeking all that is true. Wisdom lies within honesty, not deception.

Realizing that education is never-ending. Even death is a final lesson.

Learning from Mother Nature. Her wisdom is infinite.

The greatest obstacle to the internal nature is the mind. If it relies on logic such as the white man's mind, the domain of the inner nature is inaccessible. The simple fact is man does not challenge the wisdom of the Holy Mystery.

—TURTLEHEART, TETON SIOUX

September 1

*Whenever the white man treats the
Indian as they treat each other, then
we will have no more wars. We shall
all be alike—brothers or one father
and one another, with one sky above
us and one country around us, and
one government for all.*

—Chief Joseph
(Hin-mah-too-yah-lat-kekt) Nez Perce,
1840–1904

Did You Know?

Inuit women used to tattoo their faces
to enhance their beauty and to signify
their readiness to marry.

September 2

The people were put upon this world to learn of themselves and of their brothers and sisters. We are these People. We are the Fallen Star. Our laws of men change with our understanding of them. Only the laws of the Spirit remain always the same.

—WHITE WOLF,
CROW

Did You Know?

Fall harvest festivals, feasts, and giving-thanks celebrations have been a part of Native tradition for thousands of years.

September 3

If an Apache had allowed his aged parents to suffer for food or shelter, if he had neglected or abused the sick, if he had profaned our religion, or had been unfaithful, he might be banished from the tribe.

—GOYATHLAY (GERONIMO),
APACHE MEDICINE MAN AND WAR CHIEF,
1829–1909

In Remembrance

On this day in 1783, an entire Brulé village was massacred by 1,300 soldiers avenging the death of 30 soldiers who were killed for murdering Conquering Bear, the Brulé chief, during an argument over livestock.

September 4

He gains success and avoids failure by learning how others succeeded or failed, and without trouble to himself.

—CROW TEACHING

Did You Know?

The Plains tribes would lay their dead on elevated platforms or in treetops so the bodies would be close to the Great Spirit and safe from preying animals.

September 5

Finish what you begin.
Those who leave things half
done get boils on their heads.
Do you want boils on your head?

—SEVENKA QOYAWAYMA,
HOPI, 1964

In Remembrance

Of Crazy Horse, who died September 5, 1877, at Fort Robinson, Nebraska.

September 6

There are four ways in which you may go, if you are going somewhere. The first is to go immediately on first thought. That is not right. Think about it. This will make it the second way. Then think about it a third time, but don't go away yet. Then on the fourth consideration, go and it will be all right. Thus you will be safe. Sometimes wait a day in between considerations of your problems.

—DIABLO,
WHITE MOUNTAIN APACHE, 1942

September 7

For an important marriage the chief presided, aided by his wife. He passed a pipe around the room so each could share a smoke in common. In this way families were publically united to banish any past or future disagreement and thus stood as "one united." The chief then gave the couple an oration of his advice, pointing out the good characteristics of each, and then offered his congratulations to them for a happy future.

—MOURNING DOVE (CHRISTINE QUINTASKET),
SALISH, 1888–1936

September 8

But if the vision was true and mighty, and I know, it is true and mighty yet; for such things are of the spirit, and it is in the darkness of their eyes that men get lost.

—BLACK ELK,
OGLALA SIOUX, 1863–1950

On This Date in
Native American History

September 8, 1565: The first permanent European colony was established at St. Augustine, Florida, in what will eventually become the United States of America.

September 9

The Indian believes profoundly in silence—the sign of a perfect equilibrium. Silence is the absolute poise or balance of body, mind and spirit. The man who preserves his selfhood is ever calm and unshaken by the storms of existence . . . What are the fruits of silence? They are self-control, true courage or endurance, patience, dignity, and reverence. Silence is the cornerstone of character.

—OHIYESA (CHARLES EASTMAN),
SANTEE SIOUX, 1858–1939

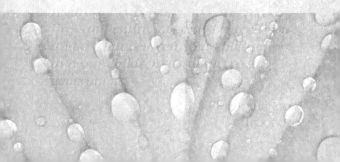

September 10

The frog does not drink up
the pond in which he lives.

—TETON SIOUX PROVERB

Did You Know?

Cotton cloth was first invented by American Indians.

September 11

*The honor of the people lies in
the moccasin tracks of the women . . .
No people goes down until their
women are weak and dishonored,
or dead upon the ground.*

—Anonymous male Sioux

Did You Know?

A give-away is a common custom among many Native nations. Unlike other cultures where a person is given gifts for their accomplishments, many Native societies believe gifts are given by the person being honored. The more revered they are, the more they give. For some, the chief was the poorest person in the community.

September 12

*We cannot reap happiness while
wallowing in the mire of immaturity,
because immaturity fosters emotional
chaos, self-degradation, and depravity.*

—MOSES SHONGO,
SENECA

On This Date in
Native American History

September 12, 1962: Ojibway artist
Norval Morrisseau exhibited his now-
famous paintings at the Pollock Gallery
(Toronto) for the very first time.

September 13

So live your life that the fear of death can never enter your heart.

—TECUMSEH,
SHAWNEE, 1768–1813

On This Date in
Native American History

The American have not yet defeated us by land; neither are we sure that they have done so by water; we therefore, wish to remain here, and fight our enemy, if they should make an appearance. If they defeat us, we will then retreat with our father.

You have got the arms and ammunition which our great father sent for his red children. If you have an idea of going away, give them to us, and you may go and welcome.

—TECUMSEH, SHAWNEE,
SPEAKING TO COLONEL HENRY PROCTOR,
WHO WANTED TECUMSEH AND HIS PEOPLE
TO RETREAT WITH THE BRITISH INTO CANADA,
SEPTEMBER 13, 1813

September 14

When you see a new trail or a
footprint you do not know, follow
it to the point of knowing.

—Uncheedah,
Santee Sioux

On This Date in
Native American History

September 14, 1972: Noted golfer, Notah Begay III, the very first Native American Indian to join a PGA Tour, was born.

Red Road Lesson 9
The Moon

The moon, referred to as Grandmother Moon by various American Indian people, pertains to female fertility, night activities, dreams, and, for most, lunar calendars and weather.

It is necessary to not only learn about the moon as a celestial entity, but to also celebrate her rotations, rhythms, and importance to the world as a whole. Be sure to gaze upon her full face each month and memorialize her grand beauty. Use this time to reflect on your life, and to plan for your future.

My father explained this to me. "All things in this world," he said, "have souls or spirits. The sky has a spirit, the clouds have spirits; the sun and moon have spirits; so have animals, trees, grass, water, stones—everything."

—EDWARD GOODBIRD,
HIDATSA, 1914

September 15

Have patience.
All things change in due time.
Wishing cannot bring autumn
glory nor cause winter to cease.

—GINALY-LI, CHEROKEE

Did You Know?

Tribes often have two names. One is the name they call themselves, and the second is the name the non–Native Indians called them (and usually, still use when referring to them). Below are just a few alternative tribal names:

Common name	Tribal name
Anadarko	Nadaco
Cayuga	Kweniogwen
Cherokee	Tsalagi
Crow	Absaroke
Iowa	Pahodja
Kickapoo	Kiwigapawa
Lumbee	Cheraw
Navajo	Dineh
Shawnee	Savannah

September 16

Every part of this Earth is sacred to my people, every shining pine needle, every sandy shore, every mist in the dark woods, every meadow, every humming insect . . .

—Chief Seattle (Seathl),
Duwamish-Suquamish, 1785–1866

Did You Know?

Interested in attending a powwow? There are basic guidelines:

Listen to the Master of Ceremonies.

Remove your hat, and stand when others do.

Seats inside the circles are reserved for performers.

Do not dress "like an Indian" or mimic the Native people.

Do not touch a person's regalia (outfit) without permission.

If you are asked to dance by an elder, do so. Saying no is disrespectful.

Pick up your trash.

Support the people via donations or by purchasing items at vending areas.

September 17

It is senseless to fight when you cannot hope to win.

—GOYATHLAY (GERONIMO),
APACHE MEDICINE MAN AND WAR
CHIEF, 1829–1909

Did You Know?

The American Indian Historical Society was founded in 1964 to educate the public about Native American people and culture.

September 18

The entire Creation still follows . . . Instructions of Life. The Tree, the fruits, they never fail. They never make a mistake to bring their fruits in their season. The animals never make a mistake. They still live as they were created. Among the Creation . . . Life, the circle, a measurement with no beginning and no ending.

—PHILLIP DEERE,
MUSKOGEE-CREEK, 1977

September 19

Guard your tongue in youth, and in age you may mature a thought that will be of service to your people.

—WABASHA,
MDEWAKANTON SIOUX, 19TH CENTURY

Did You Know?

A community college in San Francisco, California, was named Ohlone College in 1967 in honor of the Ohlone Indians, who once resided on the land the school is occupying.

September 20

To "make medicine" is to engage upon a special period of fasting, thanksgiving, prayer and self-denial, even of self-torture. The procedure is entirely a devotional exercise. The purpose is to subdue the passions of the flesh and to improve the spiritual self. The bodily abstinence and the mental concentration upon lofty thoughts cleanses both the body and the soul and puts them into or keeps them in health. Then the individual mind gets closer toward conformity with the mind of the Great Medicine above us.

—WOODEN LEG,
CHEYENNE, LATE 19TH CENTURY

September 21

*Why would you devote yourselves,
your women, and your
children to destruction?*

—BETWEEN THE LOGS,
WYANDOT, ABOUT 1812

Did You Know?

A sweat lodge is a ceremonial building made of twigs, animal hides, and/or tree bark, and is used for purification purposes. Water is poured over hot rocks and the construction captures and holds steam much like a sauna. Sweat lodges were common in Native American cultures and are still used today.

September 22

You say that you are sent to instruct us how to worship the Great Spirit agreeably to his mind; and if we do not take hold of the religion which you white people teach we shall be unhappy hereafter? You say that you are right, and we are lost. How do you know this to be true? We understand that your religion is written in a book. If it was intended for us as well as for you, why has not the Great Spirit given it to us; and not only to us, but why did he not give our forefathers the knowledge of that book, with the means of understanding it rightly?

—RED JACKET (SAGOYEWATHA),
SENECA, ABOUT 1790

September 23

No talk is ever given without first indicating your humility. "I am an ignorant man; I am a poor man . . ."—all the talks start this way. "I don't know nearly as much as you men sitting around here, but I would like to offer my humble opinion . . ."—and then he'll knock you down with logic and wisdom.

—ALLEN QUETONE,
KIOWA, 1974

September 24

Death will come, and always comes out of season. It is the command of the Great Spirit, and all nations and people must obey.

—BLACK ELK,
OGLALA SIOUX, 1863–1950

Did You Know?

For more than 4,000 years, Inuits in the Arctic have trained dogs to pull loaded sleds.

September 25

There are the springs of the Great Spirit . . . To bathe in them gives new life; to drink them cures every bodily ill.

—ARAPAHO INDIAN GUIDE

Did You Know?

A "pahos" is a prayer stick, or prayer feathers, used by the Hopi. Pahos are used during prayer and taken to sacred shrines, and are ritually smudged.

September 26

The many moons and sunny days we have lived here will long be remembered by us. The Great Spirit has smiled upon us and made us glad. But we have agreed to go. We go to a country we know little of. Our home will be beyond a great river on the way to the setting sun. We will build our wigwams there in another land . . . The men we leave here in possession of these lands cannot say Keokuk or his people ever took up the tomahawk . . . In peace we bid you goodbye . . . If you come see us, we will gladly welcome you.

—KEOKUK, A SAUK TRIBAL LEADER, WHO SIGNED A NUMBER OF TREATIES WITH THE UNITED STATES GOVERNMENT GIVING IT VARIOUS TRACTS OF LAND IN EXCHANGE FOR RESERVATION LAND AND NECESSITIES FOR HIS PEOPLE. THIS SPEECH WAS GIVEN WHEN HIS PEOPLE WERE TOLD THEY WOULD HAVE TO RELOCATE WEST OF THE MISSISSIPPI RIVER, SEPTEMBER 26, 1833

September 27

God Almighty has made us all.

— RED CLOUD (MAKHPIYA-LUTA),
OGLALA SIOUX CHIEF

Did You Know?

In 1923, John Levi became the first
Native American to be named to the
All-America football team.

September 28

We respected our old people above all others in the tribe. To live to be so old they must have been brave and strong, and good fighters, and we aspired to be like them. We never allowed our old people to want for anything . . . We looked upon our old people as demigods of a kind, we loved them deeply. They were all our fathers.

—BUFFALO CHILD LONG LANCE,
1890–1932

September 29

If an innocent man doesn't get angry, he'll live a long while. A guilty man will get sick because of bad thoughts, a bad conscience.

—TRADITIONAL HOPI TEACHING

A Native to Know

Abenaki filmmaker Alanis Obomsawin was born in 1932 and raised on the Odanak Abenaki Reserve in Quebec. She first became a singer, and then an actress, and then turned to documentary filmmaking. Her film, *Kanehsatake: 270 Years of Resistance*, won several international awards.

September 30

We were taught to believe that the Great Spirit sees and hears everything, and that he never forgets; that hereafter he will give every man a spirit-home according to his deserts . . . This I believe, and all my people believe the same.

—CHIEF JOSEPH
(HIN-MAH-TOO-YAH-LAT-KEKT) NEZ PERCE,
1840–1904

A Native to Know

He received a vision as a young boy and saw that the buffalo would be destroyed, and so would the Crow way of life. He was an honored warrior and quickly rose to the rank of chief. Chief Plenty Coups is considered the last chief to gain the status of "chief" in the traditional Crow manner.

THE WESTERN
JOURNEY OF AUTUMN

Autumn is a time for introspection, harvest, and thankfulness. As the growing season comes to an end, we look to the west, the direction of sundown, and know that the blackness of winter is approaching. Use this time to reflect, to remember our past and those who crossed over before us. Autumn is also for sharing, for donating time and money to charity, and for forgiving those who need forgiveness. Set aside grievances and focus on tomorrow.

Direction: West
Season: Autumn
Color: Black

Of all the animals the horse is the best friend of the Indian, for without it he could not go on long journeys. A horse is the Indian's most valuable piece of property. If an Indian wishes to gain something, he promises that if the horse will help him he will paint it with native dye, that all may see that help has come to him through the aid of his horse.

—BRAVE BUFFALO,
TETON SIOUX, LATE 19TH CENTURY

OCTOBER

OCTOBER PASSAMAQUODDY MOON:
HARVEST MOON

Red Road Ethic 10
Practice Forgiveness

Your journey upon the Red Road will be filled with acts requiring forgiveness—forgiveness of others and forgiveness of yourself. Mindfully practice this incredible act of humanity and the Red Road will be an easy path to follow. Also, absolution breeds the same in others. Be quick to forgive and others will grant you the same kindness.

Indians love their friends and kindred, and treat them with kindness.

—CORNPLANTER,
SENECA, 1736–1836

October 1

*Peace . . . comes within the souls of
men when they realize their relationship, their oneness, with the universe
and all its powers, and when they
realize that at the center of the
Universe dwells Wakan-Tanka, and
that this center is really everywhere,
it is within each of us.*

—BLACK ELK,
OGLALA SIOUX, 1863–1950

On This Date in
Native American History

October 1, 1969: Parents of American
Indian children attempted to enroll
their children in a desegregated school
in South Carolina. Federal marshals
and school officials forced the families
to exit the premises or be faced with
criminal charges.

October 2

*God said he was the Father and the
Earth was the Mother of mankind;
that nature was the law; that the animals and fish and plants obeyed
nature and that man only was sinful.
This is the old law.*

—Smowhala,
Wanapum

On This Date in
Native American History

October 2, 1978: The Federal Acknow-
ledgment of Indian Tribes Act was
passed through Congress. The purpose
of the legislation is to acknowledge the
actual existence of certain American
Indian tribes within the United States.

October 3

I wonder if the ground has anything to say? I wonder if the ground is listening to what is said? I wonder if the ground would come alive and what is on it? Though I hear what the ground says. The ground says, It is the Great Spirit that placed me here. The Great Spirit tells me to take care of the Indians, to feel them aright. The Great Spirit appointed the roots to feed the Indians on. The water says the same thing. The Great Spirit directs me, Feed the Indians well. The grass says the same thing, Feed the Indians well. The ground, water and grass say, The Great Spirit has given us names. We have these names and hold these names. The ground says, The Great Spirit has placed me here to produce all that grows on me, trees and fruit. The same way the ground says, It was from me man was made. The Great Spirit, in placing men on the Earth, desired them to take good care of the ground and do each other no harm . . .

—CHIEF YOUNG, CAYUSE, 1855

October 4

There is something that whispers to me it would be prudent to listen to offers of peace.

—LITTLE TURTLE,
MIAMI, 1794

A Native to Know

Little Turtle was born in Indiana in 1752 but was raised in Ohio. He was a brave warrior and became leader of the Miamis by 1790. He struggled with the whites and tried to secure his land for his people, and even united with the Wyandots, Shawnees, and Delawares. But after the Battle of Fallen Timbers, he opted to fight for peace, not war.

October 5

*Too many have strayed from the path
shown to us by the Great Spirit.*

—SEQUICHIE GRANDFATHER

In Remembrance

Of Tecumseh, the great Shawnee tribal
leader, who worked to forge an alliance
among Native Americans to fight for
land and basic rights of their people. He
died on October 5, 1813, in battle with
U.S. forces.

October 6

*It is better for us to die like warriors
than to diminish away by inches.
The cause of the red men is just, and
I hope that the [Creator] who
governs everything will favor us.*

—CORNSTALK,
SHAWNEE, 1700s

Did You Know?

"Connecticut" is from the Mohican
word meaning "long river place."

October 7

*The chastisement of God is worse
than any physical pain or sickness.*

—ROSALIO MOISES,
YAQUI

Did You Know?

Virginia Rosemyre, Gabrielino-Serrano,
was an accomplished artist and produced several hundred oil paintings in
her lifetime. She lived from 1875 to 1921.

October 8

*Do not speak of evil, for it creates
curiosity in the minds of the young.*

—LAKOTA SIOUX PROVERB

Did You Know?

More than 8,000 Indians served in
World War I, 25,000 in World War II,
41,000 in Vietnam, and 24,000 in
Operation Desert Storm.

October 9

*Walk the good road . . . Be dutiful,
respectful, gentle and modest . . .
Be strong with the warm,
strong heart of the earth.*

—Anonymous male Sioux

On This Date in
Native American History

October 9, 1813: Major Thomas Rowland described the death of Tecumseh at the battle of the Thames: "There was something so majestic, so dignified, and yet so mild, in his countenance as he lay stretched on the ground, where a few minutes before he rallied his men to the fight, that while gazing on him with admiration and pity, I forgot he was a savage. He had such a countenance as I shall never forget. He had received a wound in the arm, and had it bound up, before he received the mortal wound."

October 10

We must be united . . . We must
smoke the same pipe . . . We must
fight each other's battles . . .
and more than that,
we must love the Great Spirit.

—Tecumseh, Shawnee, 1768–1813

Did You Know?

A Roadman is a peyote holy man
of the Native American church.

October 11

It was supposed that lost spirits were roving about everywhere in the invisible air, waiting for children to find them if they searched long and patiently enough. The spirit sang its spiritual song for the child to memorize and use when calling upon the spirit guardian as an adult.

—Mourning Dove (Christine Quintasket), Salish, 1888–1936

October 12

Your mind must never be like a tipi.
Leave the entrance flap open so that
the fresh air can enter and clear out
the smoke of confusion.

—CHIEF EAGLE,
TETON SIOUX

On This Date in
Native American History

October 12, 1492: Christopher Colum-
bus accidentally lands in the Bahamas.

October 13

*We may misunderstand,
but we do not misexperience.*

—VINE DELORIA JR.,
LAKOTA, STANDING ROCK SIOUX

A Native to Know

Cree musician Buffy Sainte-Marie was raised by a Micmac couple in Canada. She was world-famous by the 1970s for her singing and songwriting, especially protest songs like "Now That the Buffalo's Gone."

October 14

*The song of the bird in the open
tree is the one that brings true music
to the ear, while that of the one in
the cage is but a sad imitation.*

—"Old Keyam" (Edward Ahenakew),
Plains Cree

On This Date in
Native American History

October 14, 1964: Billy Mills, Sioux,
won the Olympic Gold Medal for the
10,000-meter run in record time—28
minutes and 24.04 seconds—in Tokyo.
With his victory came much publicity
and distinction. In the 100-year history
of the Olympic games, Mills was the
first Native American Indian to win the
event.

Red Road Lesson 10
Turtle Island

Northern America has been called Turtle Island by many Native tribes for generations. The reference stems from a belief that the continent was placed upon the Great Turtle's back. Drawings of North America often depict the land as a turtle, and some use the tortoise as a representation of their tribes.

Indians love their friends and kindred, and treat them with kindness.

—CORNPLANTER,
SENECA, 1736–1836

October 15

*In our language there is no word to
say inferior or superiority or equality
because we are all equal . . .*

—ALANIS OBOMSAWIN,
ABENAKI

On This Date in
Native American History

October 15, 1925: *The Vanishing American*, a controversial motion picture exploring the mismanagement and corruption of reservations and how this affects the American Indian, premiered in New York City. This sympathetic view of indigenous people was not completely well received by the American public, and many debated not only the condition of the American Indian, but also what should be done with them.

October 16

*I can tell my children that the way
to get honor is to go to work and
be good men and women.*

—CHIEF RUNNING BIRD,
KIOWA

Did You Know?

When a young hunter killed his first
deer, seal, buffalo, or other large
animal meant for consumption, the
community usually held a special ceremony in his honor.

October 17

Certain small ways and observances sometimes have connection with large and more profound ideas.

—LUTHER STANDING BEAR,
OGLALA SIOUX, 1868–1937

A Native to Know

Pretty Shield, Crow, was born in 1857. She became an important medicine woman and an outspoken advocate for her people's traditional way of life.

October 18

I'm the only one who's responsible for my soul, if I don't do the right thing here. I'm at fault, not him, not the church, not that mountain over there or the sun. This is the way they teach Indian religion. No one is going to influence you, no one is going to bring you up to your grave, but yourself.

—ALEX SALUSKIN,
YAKIMA, 1970

October 19

There are no Indians
left now but me . . .

—HUNKESNI (SITTING BULL),
SAID IN ANGER TO HIS PEOPLE FOR TURNING
OVER 10 MILLION ACRES OF RESERVATION LAND
TO THE U.S. GOVERNMENT IN 1889

On This Date in
Native American History

October 19, 1984: An amendment to the
Indian Education Act of 1972 called,
The Indian Education Amendment, was
enacted, promising to improve educational standards of Native American
children by extending programs and
allowing Indian tribes to engage in a
policy of self-determination.

October 20

*I went up to heaven and saw the Great
Spirit and all the people who had died
a long time ago. The Great Spirit told
me to come back and tell my people
they must be good and love one
another, and not fight, steal, or lie.*

—WOVOKA (JACK WILSON),
PAIUTE SPIRITUAL LEADER, 1889

On This Date in
Native American History

October 20, 1876: Satanta (White Bear)
spoke to representatives of the United
States government at Medicine Lodge
Creek. Satanta spoke of the right to raise
his children as he was raised. He asked
not to be placed on a reservation, and
said, "I have heard that you intend to
settle us on a reservation. I don't want to
settle. I love to roam over the prairies.
When we settle down we grow pale
and die." Satanta was later imprisoned
for alleged participation in murderous
raids on white frontiersmen—he committed suicide in prison in 1878.

October 21

When [I was] a child, my mother taught me . . . to kneel and pray to Usen for strength, health, wisdom, and protection.

—Goyathlay (Geronimo),
Apache medicine man and war chief,
1829–1909

A Native to Know

Wilma Mankiller was elected the first female deputy chief of the Cherokees in 1983. She was involved in the Alcatraz occupation of 1969, has taught at Dartmouth College, and has written her memoir.

October 22

An Indian respects a brave man,
but he despises a coward.
He loves a straight tongue,
but he hates a forked tongue.

—CHIEF JOSEPH,
NEZ PERCE, 1879

On This Date in
Native American History

October 22, 1844: Metis leader Louis Riel Jr. was born.

October 23

To give up when all is against you is a sign of being weak and cowardly.

—CHIEF EAGLE,
TETON SIOUX

In Remembrance

Of Chief Ten Bears, a great leader of the Yamparika Comanches, who died on October 23, 1872, following a trip to Washington, D.C., to discuss peace between his people and the United States.

October 24

My son, you are now flesh and bone of our bone. By the ceremony performed this day, every drop of white blood was washed from your veins; you were taken into the Shawnee nation . . . you were adopted into a great family.

—BLACK FISH, SHAWNEE, AT THE TRIBAL ADOPTION OF DANIEL BOONE, 1778

October 25

Standards of conduct were just as rigid as the laws of any other people, but force seldom was used to enforce good conduct. Each person was his own judge. Deceitfulness was a crime. We lived according to our own standards and principles, not for what others might think of us.

—THOMAS WILDCAT ALFORD,
SHAWNEE

October 26

*We believe that the spirit pervades all
creation and that every creature pos-
sesses a soul in some degree, though
not necessarily a soul conscious of
itself. The tree, the waterfall, the grizzly
bear, each is an embodied Force, and
as such an object of reverence.*

—OHIYESA (CHARLES EASTMAN),
SANTEE SIOUX, 1858–1939

October 27

We ask every lover of justice, is it right that a great and powerful government should, year by year, continue to demand cessions of land from weaker and dependent people, under the plea of securing homes for the homeless?

—Delegates of the Choctaw and Chickasaw Nation, about 1895

October 28

When this pipe touches your lip, may it operate as a blessing upon all my tribe. May the smoke rise like a cloud, and carry away with it all the animosities which have arisen between us.

—Black Thunder,
Fox

On This Date in
Native American History

October 28, 1871: In Edmonton, Alberta, Canada, indigenous people began a six-month sit-in at the Indian Affairs Office to protest the harsh conditions for children at reservation schools.

October 29

Marriage among my people was like traveling in a canoe. The man sat in front and paddled the canoe. The woman sat in the stern, but she steered.

—ANONYMOUS

Did You Know?

The dreamcatcher is an easily recognizable piece of Native Americana. There are two kinds of dreamcatchers. The first, for children, will include feathers and is made from willow so that it will eventually fall apart (representing the child growing out of childhood). The adult dreamcatcher is usually made with a center feather and beads. It is made of woven fiber and will last longer.

All dreamcatchers have some type of representation of the four directions as well as a spider's web, and will be made from all-natural material. The dreamcatcher is *only* to be placed on the wall above the bed of the person the dreamcatcher was made for. It must be made from hand.

October 30

*I am the Maker of heaven and
earth, the trees, lakes, rivers, and
all things else. I am the Maker
of Mankind; and because I love you,
you must do my will . . .*

—PONTIAC, OTTAWA TRIBE,
REPEATING WHAT THE GREAT
SPIRIT TOLD HIM IN 1763

On This Date in
Native American History

October 30, 1990: Congress enacted
the Native American Languages Act,
admitting that ". . . there is a wide-
spread practice of treating Native
American languages as if they were
anachronisms . . . there is a lack of
clear, comprehensive, and consistent
Federal policy on treatment of Native
American languages which has often
resulted in acts of suppression and
extermination of Native American languages and cultures . . . in conflict
with the United States policy of self-
determination for Native Americans."

October 31

*Brother: We are of the same opinion
with the people of the United States; you
consider yourselves as independent
people; we, as the original inhabitants
of this country, and sovereigns of the
soil, look upon ourselves as equally
independent, and free as any other
nation or nations. This country was
give to us by the Great Spirit above; we
wish to enjoy it*

—Thayendanegea (Joseph Brant),
Mohawk, at a council with whites, 1794

November

November Wishram Moon:
Snowy-Mountains-in-
the-Morning Moon

Red Road Ethic 11
Practice Optimism

It is easy to live within the shadow of fear, procrastination, and pessimism. But these are bad habits and stumbling blocks that keep you from experiencing life, the Red Road, and the Great Spirit. It is well known to the Native people that optimism is the key to good health. Worry makes you sick—as do bad thoughts. Replace them with happiness and optimism and you shall live a long, healthy life.

Oh hear me, Grandfather, and help us, that our generation in the future will live and walk the good road with the flowering stick of success. Also, the pipe of peace, we will offer it as we walk the good road to success. Hear me, and hear our plea . . .

—BLACK ELK,
OGLALA SIOUX, 1863–1950

November 1

*My heart laughs with joy
because I am in your presence.*

—CHITMACHAS CHIEF

On This Date in
Native American History

November 1, 1972: Hundreds of Indian activists banded together in protest at the Sioux Rosebud Reservation.

November 2

*All life was injustice . . . Lightning
found the good man and the bad;
sickness carried no respect for virtue,
and luck flitted around like the spring
butterfly. It is good to learn this in
the days of mother's milk.*

—BAD ARM,
SIOUX, 1862

Did You Know?

November is American Indian Heritage
Month.

November 3

*Happiness is not only good in itself
but it is very healthful.*

—HOPI TEACHING

A Native to Know

Billy Mills, Oglala Sioux, was born June
30, 1938, in South Dakota. He is known
for his outstanding long-distance running abilities and his accomplishments
at the 1964 Summer Olympic games in
Japan. Mills entered the 10,000-meter
run, knowing that no American has
ever won that race. Mills ran the 10,000
meter, won the Gold, and stands today
as the only Native American to do so.
The 1984 movie *Running Brave* is
based on this victory.

November 4

All life is Wakan. So also is everything which exhibits power, whether in action, as the winds and drifting clouds, or in passive endurance, as the boulder by the wayside. For even the commonest sticks and stones have a spiritual essence which must be revered as a manifestation of the all-pervading mysterious power that fills the universe.

—FRANCIS LAFLESCHE,
OSAGE

On This Date in
Native American History

November 4, 1879: William Penn Adair Rogers, Cherokee Indian, known to the world as Will Rogers, was born in Indian Territory (present-day Oklahoma).

November 5

We shall not fail . . . to nourish your hearts . . . about the renewal of our amity and the brightening of the Chain of Friendship . . .

—CANASSATEGO,
ONONDAGA, 1742

On This Date in
Native American History

November 5, 2000: Ralph Nader and Winona LaDuke continued their campaign to secure the positions of president and vice-president of the United States of America under the Green Party ticket. LaDuke, a member of the Mississippi Band of Anishinaabe (Ojibway) from the White Earth Reservation in Minnesota, received her B.A. from Harvard, serves as the director of the White Earth Land Recovery Project, is a board member of Greenpeace Action, and received the Reebok Human Rights Award in 1988.

November 6

There needs to be room in a political party for all of us, because if we actually want to get things done we've got to make room for the diversity of people.

—WINONA LADUKE, OJIBWAY,
GREEN PARTY VICE-PRESIDENTIAL CANDIDATE

On This Date in
Native American History

November 6, 1986: Ben Nighthorse Campbell was elected to the U.S. House of Representatives (Colorado). Campbell, a Northern Cheyenne Indian from Montana, is the second Native American elected to such a position.

November 7

Never be elevated above measure by success . . . nor delighted with the sweets of peace to suffer insults.

—PUSHMATAHA,
CHOCTAW TRIBAL LEADER, 1764–1824

On This Date in
Native American History

November 7, 1811: Shawnee chief, Tecumseh, and others were traveling through southern American Indian communities seeking an alliance of nations for his confederacy against the white takeover within their homelands. In his absence, his brother, Tenskwatawa was to care for the Shawnee people and was ordered by Tecumseh not to engage in battles with the whites. Knowing of Tecumseh's absence, William Henry Harrison and more than 1,000 of his men invade the village and force Tenskwatawa into battle that devastates the Shawnee. Today this fight is called "The Battle of Tippecanoe."

November 8

We first knew you a feeble plant which wanted a little earth whereon to grow. We gave it to you; and afterward, when we could have trod you under our feet, we watered and protected you; and now you have grown to be a mighty tree, whose top reaches the clouds, and whose branches overspread the whole land, whilst we, who were the tall pines of the forest, have become a feeble plant and need your protection.

—RED JACKET (SAGOYEWATHA), SENECA, C. 1752–1830

November 9

Those who know how to play can easily leap over the adversities of life. And one who knows how to sing and laugh never brews mischief.

—IGLULIK PROVERB

On This Date in Native American History

November 9, 1969: The occupation of Alcatraz, a defining moment in modern Native American history. In 1969, Indian activists, following the lead of the black civil rights movement, staged several protests. One of the most newsworthy was the occupation of Alcatraz Island, once the country's most notorious prison. The occupation, which helped American Indians achieve a visibility long denied them, was solidly based on treaty rights, and helped build a movement that continues to support members of the community to this day.

November 10

The Creator made it to be this way. An old woman shall be as a child again and her grandchildren shall care for her. For only because she is, they are.

—HANDSOME LAKE,
SENECA, C. 1735–1815

Did You Know?

"Missouri" is an Algonquin word meaning "river of big canoes."

November 11

Try to do something that is brave. That man is most successful who is foremost.

—JUMPING BULL,
HUNKPAPA SIOUX

A Native to Know

In early 1800, Sacagawea was kidnapped from her tribe, the Shoshone, by Crow Indians and sold to Mandans. She married a French fur trapper, and by the time she was 18, she had his child. She remained a captive until the fur trapper made a deal with Lewis and Clark that allowed Sacagawea to be the interpreter and guide they needed to lead them through the wild terrain. Sacagawea and her child made history when they embarked on the lengthy journey. She was eventually reunited with her Shoshone people.

November 12

Brother, listen to us, your younger brothers. As we see something in your eyes that looks dissatisfaction, we now clear them. You have credited bad stories against us. We clean your ears, that you may hear better hereafter. We wish to remove every thing bad from your heart, that you may be as good as your ancestors. We saw you coming with an uplifted tomahawk in your hand. We now take it from you, and throw it up to God. Brother, as you are a warrior, take hold of this chain of friendship, and let us think no more of war, in pity of our old men, women, and children. We, too, are warriors.

—RED HAWK, SHAWNEE,
ADDRESSING BRITISH COLONEL HENRY BOUQUET,
NOVEMBER 12, 1764

November 13

That people will continue longest in the enjoyment of peace who timely prepare to vindicate themselves and manifest a determination to protect themselves whenever they are wronged.

—TECUMSEH,
SHAWNEE, 1768–1813

November 14

Be happy in order to live long.
Worry makes you sick.

—HOPI TEACHING

Did You Know?

Buffalo skulls were used as a sacred decoration by many Plains tribes during celebrations and ceremonies such as the Sun Dance.

Red Road Lesson 11
Children Are the Future

Children are gifts of the Creator and of ourselves. By raising them to the best of our ability, we are reciprocating that gift and showing our thankfulness for life and for the blessings of the Great Spirit. This requires much time, love, forgiveness, and understanding on the part of the parents and grandparents—but the rewards for the child (and for the community as a whole) are immeasurable.

Also, it is not enough to raise your own children and grandchildren. You should bestow what you can to *all* children of the Earth.

It is strictly believed and understood by the Sioux that a child is the greatest gift from Wakan Tanka in response to many devout prayers, sacrifices, and promises. Therefore the child is considered "sent by Wakan Tanka" through some element—namely the element of human nature.

—Robert Higheagle,
Teton Sioux, early 20th century

November 15

Hold on to what is good, even if it is a handful of dirt. Hold on to what you believe, even if it is a tree that stands by itself. Hold on to what you must do, even if it is a long way from here. Hold on to life, even if it is easier to let go. Hold on to my hand, even if I have gone away from you.

—PUEBLO BLESSING

A Native to Know

Clyde Bellecourt, Ojibway, was born on the White Earth Reservation in Minnesota in 1939. He is one of the founders of the American Indian Movement and is instrumental in many Native activist projects to this day.

November 16

As there is no alternative between a falsehood and a lie, they (the American Indian) usually tell any person, you "lie," as a friendly negative to a reputed truth.

—ADAIR

On This Date in Native American History

November 16, 1990: Congress passed the Native American Graves Protection and Repatriation Act.

November 17

When we go hunting, it is not our arrow that kills the moose, however powerful the bow; it is nature that kills him.

—BEDAGI (BIG THUNDER),
WABANAKÍ ALGONQUIN, LATE 19TH CENTURY

On This Date in
Native American History

November 17, 1945: Tlingit filmmaker Carol Geddes was born.

November 18

It is our desire that we and you should be as one heart, one mind, and one body, thus becoming one people, entertaining a mutual love and regard for each other, to be preserved firm and entire, not only between you and us, but between your children and our children, to all succeeding generations.

—KANICKHUNGO,
IROQUOIS

November 19

You have spoken words of comfort . . . as though the Great Spirit was speaking through you.

—LITTLE BEAVER

On This Date in Native American History

November 19, 1986: The American Indian Vietnam Plaque, commemorating the diligent service of nearly 43,000 Native American Indians who served in the Vietnam war, was dedicated at Arlington National Cemetery.

November 20

Might I behold thee,
Might I know thee,
Might I consider thee,
Might I understand thee,
O Lord of the universe.

—INCA SAYING

On This Date in
Native American History

November 20, 1890: The stronghold plateau was on the Pine Ridge Reservation. Wovoka had his Ghost Dance vision in 1889, and the prophecy soon caught on and swept across the West. The dance was soon outlawed by the United States government, because they thought the dance would inspire the Sioux to rise up and fight. The people started a journey to Pine Ridge to learn the prophecy and learn the dance throughout early and mid 1890. By November 20, over 3,000 people had made the pilgrimage.

November 21

*We bury them from sight for-
ever and plant again the tree.*

—DEKANAWIDAH,
IROQUOIS, C. 1300

A Native to Know

Dekanawidah, a peaceful prophet, is best known as the
author of the Great Law of the
Iroquois Confederacy, one of
the earliest constitutions in the
country, which established a
system of justice and law
administered by chiefs of various nations. Known for his
charisma, intelligence, and honesty, Dekanawidah brought
unity and brotherhood to many
of his neighboring nations.

November 22

If the Indian loves,
he speaks the truth;
but if he does not,
he is silent.

—TECUMSEH,
SHAWNEE, 1808

Did You Know?

Just as little girls today play
with miniature doll houses,
little girls of the Plains tribes
often played with miniature
versions of tipis.

November 23

The whole world belongs to Asga Ya Galun Lati, the Great Spirit.

—CHEROKEE ADAGE

A Native to Know

Lucy Lewis, Hopi-Tewa, born in 1895, is ranked as one of the best Pueblo potters of the 20th century. She won numerous awards and honors in many of the exhibitions she entered after learning pottery making from her aunt. Since her death in 1992, her work has been carried on by her daughters and granddaughters.

November 24

Let me do the right things for my people. Not for the sake of merit, but because of the sacrifice of my people in this land which belongs to them.

—Teton Sioux vision quest prayer

In Remembrance

Of Mohawk Indian Joseph Brant (also referred to as Captain Brant or Brandt), who crossed over on November 24, 1807.

November 25

*You said you would enlarge
the fire . . . add more fuel
to make it brighter.*

—CANASSATEGO, ONONDAGA, 1742

A Native to Know

Canassatego was chief of the
Onondaga Nation, one of the tribes
unified as the Five Nations. The
Native Confederacy was greatly
admired by many of America's
Founding Fathers, including Benjamin Franklin, and it was Canassatego who advised the colonists to
unite on a Haudenosaunee model of
government. The Constitution of the
United States is based on this model.

November 26

*While feeling compassion for you
in the sweetness of our response,
we wonder at the anxieties and
cares which you give yourself . . .*

—GASPESIAN CHIEF

On This Date in
Native American History

November 26, 1991: The Custer
Battlefield National Monument in
Montana, the site of "Custer's Last
Stand" was renamed the Little
Bighorn Battlefield Monument.

November 27

*The Great Spirit knows that
I have spoken the truth.*

—STRUCK BY THE REE,
YANKTON SIOUX, 1865

A Native to Know

Hiawatha helped to organize five separate Iroquoian tribes into one confederacy known as the Five Nations. His courageous work is legendary, and to some, has even reached mythological proportions. Hiawatha is known today as an intelligent, innovative leader who succeeded in uniting nations that otherwise would have been at war.

November 28

*You can't wake a person
who is pretending to be asleep.*

—NAVAJO PROVERB

On This Date in
Native American History

November 28, 1989: The Native
American Grave Protection and
Repatriation Act was signed into law
by President George Bush. Hundreds
of thousands of pieces of Native
American human remains, cultural
pieces, and funeral objects are held
by museums and universities across
the country, and this act requires the
return of those remains and items
that are attached to a particular tribe.

November 29

No person among us desires any other reward for performing a brave and worthy action, but the consciousness of having served his nation!

—THAYENDANEGEA,
(JOSEPH BRANT), MOHAWK, 1741–1807

In Remembrance

On the morning of November 29, 1864, Colonel John Chivington led a regiment of 700 volunteer militiamen into a sleeping Cheyenne and Arapaho village at Sand Creek, Colorado. Though their leader, Black Kettle, flew the American flag above his teepee, symbolizing passiveness and peace and he raised the white flag of surrender and instructed his people to stand under the post to prove to the soldiers that they were unarmed and not hostile, Chivington and his men viciously murdered 200 to 600 people—mostly women, children, and the elderly—and only a handful of men who were not participating in the hunting expedition escaped.

November 30

"To hi ge se s di"
means "peace on earth."

—Cherokee

Did You Know?

In many tribal communities it was the grandparents who instructed the child, and the parents who worked and hunted for the family. The grandparents taught tribal laws, creation stories, histories, and wisdom through stories.

Red Road Ethic 12
Take What You Need, Leave the Rest Be

There is nothing placed upon this Earth that deserves to be destroyed or wasted for the purpose of human convenience. To destroy trees and leave them unused simply because they blocked the view of the garden, or to kill animals only for their fur, is not a rightful way to share the world with another. To waste and discard something due to your own selfishness is an act that goes against the Creator, and strays you from the Red Road.

Now tell me this one little thing, if thou hast any sense: Which of these two is the wisest and happiest—he who labours without ceasing and only obtains, and that with great trouble, enough to live on, or he who rests in comfort and finds all that he needs in the pleasure of hunting and fishing?

—GASPESIAN CHIEF

DECEMBER

DECEMBER ANISHINAABE MOON:
SMALL SPIRITS MOON

Winter—known as Wicta in Yuchi—
is upon us.

December 1

A long time ago the Creator came to Turtle Island and said to the Red People, You will be the keepers of the Mother Earth. Among you I will give the wisdom about Nature, about the interconnectedness of all things, about balance and about living in harmony. You Red People will see the secrets of Nature. You will live in hardship and the blessing of this is you will stay close to the Creator. The day will come when you will need to share the secrets with other people of the earth because they will stray from their Spiritual ways. The time to start sharing is today.

—DON COYHIS,
MOHICAN

December 2

Some of you think an Indian is like a wild animal. This is a great mistake.

—CHIEF JOSEPH
(HIN-MAH-TOO-YAH-LAT-KEKT), NEZ PERCE, 1879,
ADDRESSING POLITICIANS IN WASHINGTON, D.C.

On This Date in
Native American History

December 2, 1987: The U.S. House of Representatives passed legislation to commemorate the centennial anniversary of the forced removal of the Cherokees from their eastern homelands—an event that cost the lives of approximately 4,000 people and is known as the Trail of Tears.

December 3

Face the rising sun with a cheerful spirit, as did our ancestors in the days of plenty. Their rain fell on all the land. But in these evil days it falls only on the fields of the faithful.

—WHITE BUFFALO CALF WOMAN,
TETON SIOUX

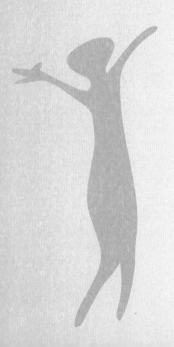

December 4

We humans must come again to a moral comprehension of the earth and air. We must live according to the principle of a land ethic. The alternative is that we shall not live at all.

—N. Scott Momaday,
Kiowa, 1970

A Native to Know

John Trudell, Santee Sioux, is a passionate activist for his people. He participated in the occupation of Alcatraz Island, joined the American Indian Movement in 1970, and participated in the 1972 Trail of Broken Treaties. He's served as consultant and actor in Native American film, and in 1992 released a record album, *AKA Graffiti Man*.

December 5

*Great Spirit . . . To the center of the
world you have taken me and showed
me the goodness and the beauty and
the strangeness of the greening earth . . .
you have shown me, and I have seen.*

—BLACK ELK,
OGLALA SIOUX, 1863–1950

December 6

*Rise to the dignity and grandeur of
your honored position . . . shake off
the base fetters of the bad spirit . . .*

—Keokuk

Did You Know?

"Kansas" is the Sioux word for "south
wind people."

December 7

How inhuman it was in those wretches to come into a country where nature shone in beauty, spreading her wings over the vast continent, sheltering beneath her shades these natural sons of an Almighty Being, that shone in grandeur and lustre like stars of the first magnitude in the heavenly world; whose virtues far surpassed their more enlightened foes, notwithstanding their pretended zeal for religion and virtues.

—WILLIAM APESS,
PEQUOT, JANUARY 6, 1836

December 8

When I caught any kind of bird, when I killed I saw that life went out with its blood. This taught me for what purpose I am here. I came into this world to die. My body is only to hold a spirit life. Should my blood be sprinkled I want no wounds from behind. Death should come fronting me.

—Toohoolhoolzote,
Nez Perce chief, mid-19th century

December 9

The Indian was a religious man from his mother's womb. From the moment of her recognition of the fact of conception to the end of the second year of life, which was the ordinary duration of lactation, the mother's spiritual influence counted for most. Her attitude and secret meditations must be such as to instill into the receptive soul of the unborn child the love of the "Great Mystery" and a sense of brotherhood with all creation.

—OHIYESA (CHARLES EASTMAN),
SANTEE SIOUX, 1858–1939

On This Date in Native American History

December 9, 1993: Sisters Marie and Carrie Dann, from the Western Shoshone nation were awarded the 1993 Right Livelihood Award (sometimes called "the other Nobel Peace Prize") and a monetary prize for their "courage and perseverance in asserting the rights of indigenous people to their land."

December 10

The trees, the animals, are all
where He has stopped, and the
Indian thinks of these places and
sends his prayers there to reach the
place where God has stopped and
win help and a blessing.

—OLD DAKOTA WISEMAN

On This Date in
Native American History

December 10, 1992: For the first time
in United Nations history, indigenous
people were invited to participate in
the UN General Assembly. Over 200
tribal representatives gathered in New
York City. Arvol Looking Horse,
keeper of the Lakota sacred pipe, initi-
ated the event with a prayer.

December 11

*The Indian loved to worship. From birth
to death he revered his surroundings.
He considered himself born in the lux-
urious lap of Mother Earth, and no
place to him was humble.*

—LUTHER STANDING BEAR,
OGLALA SIOUX, 1868–1937

On This Date in
Native American History

December 11, 2000: Various Native
American Indians, including the same
Sioux tribe once led by the legendary
leader Crazy Horse, continued their
demonstrations and protests at Liz
Claiborne headquarters to block the
company from using the Crazy Horse
name on its product line. The Native
people claim Liz Claiborne exploits
the name, legend, and image of their
heroic ancestor, and they do not give
their permission to use his name or
likeness to sell products.

December 12

Your words circle like soaring birds which never land. I will try to catch them and take them back for my people to hear.

—BLUE JACKET (WEYAPIERSENWAH), SHAWNEE, 1791

Did You Know?

Ed Morrissette (Ojibway) was the first Native American inducted into the Softball Hall of Fame.

December 13

In my early days I was eager to learn and to do things, and therefore I learned quickly.

—HUNKESNI (SITTING BULL),
HUNKPAPA SIOUX, 1831–1890

Did You Know?

A wampum was an important piece of Native culture. Made from polished shell or glass and then bound together to form a belt or strands, the wampum was a historical archive, a trading item, and a method of communication. If a red belt was given at a peace conference between two nations, it meant war. White meant peace.

December 14

This brings rest to my heart.
I feel like a leaf after a storm,
when the wind is still.

—PETALASHARO,
PAWNEE

On This Date in
Native American History

December 14, 1985: Wilma Mankiller was sworn into the Oklahoma Cherokee Nation Council as principal chief, becoming the first woman in modern history to lead a large tribe, and the very first to head the Cherokee Nation.

Red Road Lesson 12
The Importance of Dance

For generations upon generations, dance has played a significant role in the spiritual and cultural life of Native peoples from all over the American continent. It may represent an event such as the end of a harvest, or it may symbolize a spiritual legend or teaching.

Dancers are taught not only the meaning of the dance, but the meaning of every element within the dance—such as the custom, the steps, the cultural history, and the decoration of the community event. Examples of such events include the Corn Dance, the Butterfly Dance, the Hoop Dance, and the Sunrise Dance.

It is a strict law that bids us dance. It is a strict law that bids us distribute our property among our friends and neighbors.

—Anonymous Kwakiutl,
c. 1886

December 15

We sang songs that carried in their melodies all the sounds of nature . . .

—Anonymous American Indian

On This Date in
Native American History

December 15, 1970: Blue Lake was returned to the Taos people many years after the U.S. government seized it from them. Blue Lake was part of the Taos culture for more than 700 years and is considered sacred land.

December 16

The Great Spirit does right.
He knows what is best
for His children.

—SENECA TEACHING

Did You Know?

The First Annual Totem Awards were presented in 1993 to Native Americans who made outstanding contributions in television, theater, music, and film. Recipients include Wes Studi, Graham Greene, John Trudell, and Sheila Tousey.

December 17

*One never forgets to acknowledge
a favor, no matter how small.*

—MORAL TEACHING OF THE OMAHA

Did You Know?

Some tribes did not cut their hair
unless they were in mourning.

December 18

Day and night cannot dwell together.
Your religion was written on tables of
stone, ours was written on our hearts.

—CHIEF SEATTLE (SEATHL),
DUWAMISH-SUQUAMISH, 1785–1866

A Native to Know

Gertrude Simmons Bonnin, Sioux (Red
Bird or Zitkala-Sa), was born in 1876
(died 1938) at the Yankton Sioux
Agency. She attended Earlham College,
taught school, and in 1916 was elected
secretary of the Society of American
Indians. She relocated to Washington,
D.C., lectured, edited a periodical, and
co-wrote the Indian opera *Sun Dance*.

December 19

*The wildwood birds . . . sang in
concert, without pride, without
envy, without jealousy . . .*

—SIMON POKAGON,
POTAWATOMI, 1830–1899

On This Date in
Native American History

December 19, 2000: The Navajo Code
Talkers were recognized for their service in World War II.

December 20

*Can things go well in a land
where freedom of worship is a lie,
a hollow boast?*

*To each nation is given the light
by which it knows God, and each
finds its own way to express the
longing to serve Him . . . If a
nation does not do what is right
according to its own understanding, its power is worthless.*

—THUNDERCHILD,
PLAINS CREE, 1849–1927

December 21

*May the warm winds of heaven
blow softly upon your house.
May the Great Spirit bless all
who enter there.
May your moccasins make
happy tracks in many snows,
And may the rainbow always
touch your shoulder*

—CHEROKEE BLESSING

December 22

Youth is impulsive. When our young men grow angry at some real or imaginary wrong, and disfigure their faces with black paint, it denotes that their hearts are black, and that they are often cruel and relentless, and our old men and old women are unable to restrain them . . . Revenge by young men is considered gain, even at the cost of their own lives, but old men who stay at home in times of war, and mothers who have sons to lose, know better.

—CHIEF SEATTLE (SEATHL),
DUWAMISH-SUQUAMISH, 1785–1866

December 23

In anger the will power is charged with evil and the man becomes dangerous to himself and to others.

—OMAHA ADAGE

A Native to Know

Maria Tallchief, Osage, was born Betty Marie Tall Chief on the Indian lands of Oklahoma in 1925. At an early age she set her sights on being a star and became America's pre-eminent "prima ballerina." In 1953, President Dwight D. Eisenhower declared her "Woman of the Year." She later taught at the School for American Ballet in New York City, and in 1981 she cofounded the Chicago City Ballet. At present, Maria Tallchief is a member of the Lyric Opera of Chicago's Women's Board and she is the opera company's director of ballet. She also works with young singers in the Lyric Opera Center for American Artists.

December 24

Treat the earth well: it was not given to you by your parents, it was loaned to you by your children. We do not inherit the Earth from our Ancestors, we borrow it from our Children.

—ANCIENT INDIAN PROVERB

Did You Know?

"Ohio" is the Iroquois word for "fine (or good) river."

December 25

We also have a religion which was given to our forefathers, and has been handed down to us, their children. It teaches us to be thankful, to be united, and to love one another! We never quarrel about religion.

—Red Jacket (Sagoyewatha),
Seneca, c. 1752–1830

Did You Know?

A Croatan (or a Cro) is a person of mixed Indian, white, and black ancestry.

December 26

Develop your body, but do not neglect your mind. It is the mind that leads a man to power, not strength of body.

—CROW TEACHING

In Remembrance

The largest public execution was held in 1862 on this day in Mankato, Minnesota, where 38 Santee Sioux were hanged simultaneously for their alleged involvement in crimes committed during the Sioux Uprising. Originally, more than 300 men were condemned to death, but President Abraham Lincoln investigated the charges and allowed 38 of the sentences to stand.

December 27

First you are to think always of God,
of Wankan-Tanka. Second, you are to
use all your powers to care for your
people and especially for the poor.

—BLACK MOON,
HUNKPAPA SIOUX

Did You Know?

In traditional Cherokee culture, according to the book *Voices of Our Ancestors*
by Dhyani Ywahoo (Cherokee), a
person does not reach adulthood until
age 51.

December 28

A chief must not seek profit for himself.

—SWEET MEDICINE,
CHEYENNE

In Remembrance

Of the more than 300 Sioux Indians who crossed over on December 28, 1890, during the massacre at Wounded Knee.

December 29

It is the office of man to kindle the fire, but the part of the woman to keep it burning.

—PIMA ETHIC

Did You Know?

Montezuma lived in an elegant palace with buildings, an aviary, lush gardens, and even a private zoo.

December 30

It is always good to do good, it is said.

—S<small>AM</small> B<small>LOWSNAKE</small>, W<small>INNEBAGO</small>

Did You Know?

There are many stereotypes of American Indians that must be avoided. The truth is as follows:

- Indians do not all look alike.
- Not all Indians know Native history and culture, especially that which is not their own.
- Indians observe the religion of their choice.
- Not all Indians are alcoholics.
- "Indian-ness" is not decided by the percentage of Indian blood in your body.
- Indians do not always have an Indian name.
- Indians were not uncivilized before the white man came to the Western Hemisphere.
- Indians were not conquered.
- There are many American Indian heroes.

Web Sites

www.angelfire.com/mo/nativeamericanjrnl/page6.
html

http://www.carnegiemuseums.org/cmnh/exhibits/
north-south-east-west/iroquois/handsome_lake.html

http://cherokee-indians-of-ga-inc.0pi.com/custom2.
html (Cherokee Cultural Page)

http://www.countryroadchronicles.com/

http://www.emily.net/~schiller/ublision.html

www.falcon.jmu.edu/~ramseyil/natautb.htm

http://www.fallenmartyrs.com (Tribute To Fallen
Martyrs)

www.fortunecity.com/tinpan/oldsquire/285/quotes.
html

http://www.hallman.org/indian/scotseye.html

www.ilhawaii.net/~stony/quotes.html

http://www.ohiokids.org/obc/history/b_indianevents/
gnadenbu.html

http://www.pbs.org/wgbh/aia/part4/4h3083.html
(Cherokee letter protesting the Treaty of New Elocha)

www.unity.edu/sari/2000/acocebe/Native%20Links.
html

http://www.uvoca.ca/native-american-quote.htm

http://www.yale.edu/lawweb/avalon/ntreaty/ncase001.
htm

December 31

Strength is not the only thing we must have in the world, and, in a man or a nation, it is of little use without wisdom.

—CHACOPEE AND THE WOODEN MAN,
YANKTON SIOUX

On This Date in Native American History

December 31, 1910: The film *The Yaqui Girl*, a love story about an Indian woman and a Mexican man, was produced. James Young Deer, Winnebago, became the head of studio production soon after this film.